KU-143-152

VSSILAG
RT
1660

DUKE
OF CAMBRIDGE

MORE
LOOKING IN JUNK SHOPS

Also by John Bedford

LOOKING IN JUNK SHOPS
TALKING ABOUT TEAPOTS
THE COLLECTING MAN
STILL LOOKING FOR JUNK

MORE LOOKING IN
JUNK SHOPS

JOHN BEDFORD

Illustrated by
Susan Holland

MACDONALD · LONDON

First published in 1962 by
Max Parrish and Co Ltd

Reprinted 1962
Second edition 1964
Reprinted 1968
Reprinted 1969

SBN 356 01083 X

Published by
Macdonald & Co (Publishers) Ltd,
St Giles House, 49/50 Poland Street, London, W.1
Made and Printed in Great Britain by
Purnell & Sons Ltd, Paulton (Somerset) and London

Preliminary Chat

Twelve months ago I wrote a little volume called *Looking in Junk Shops*. It tried to offer guidance in recognising such antiques as are still collectable by the ordinary collector: and also, just for fun, in peeping at the things the rich people buy.

To everyone's surprise, including the publisher's, the first edition sold out, and although I had crammed it as full as an egg readers wrote in asking why I had left out this or made only the briefest reference to that. It sounded as though they wanted more.

So here is another collection of things come across in browsing through junk shops and sheds, wandering round salerooms and country houses, looking at collections, and gossiping with people who know what's what, even if it isn't. The book is not exactly a sequel to the first one, but a 'sib' of it: the two sit – happily, I hope – side by side, like the persons on one of those thoughtfully designed QUEEN ANNE love seats shown on page 186.

For this reason there is a change of emphasis in the subjects. Porcelain and glass were dealt with pretty fully in *Looking in Junk Shops*, but furniture not very much: this is reversed. I have also looked more closely at such things as jewellery, metalwork, and exotic things from the East. Many items briefly mentioned before are dealt with in more detail.

As in *Looking in Junk Shops* I have arranged the material in A to Z order, not because it is supposed to be an encyclopaedia but because I feel readers will find it easier to read that way. When a word in the text is given in CAPITAL LETTERS it means that it has an entry of its own: so if you are interested you simply follow the CAPITALS around. In some places I have inserted '*Looking in Junk Shops*'. If I had carried this out thoroughly, however, the whole book would have been peppered with this title; so I'm afraid that if you haven't got the first book you will either have to buy a copy or move near to someone who owns one.

If you want to find out more about the things in either book, there are READING LISTS, the second being in the nature of a supplement to the first.

I have also additionally sprinkled in here and there a few notes upon the styles of the different periods. They will, no doubt, horrify the learned, but I think they may be useful as a pointer for anyone wandering along the high-water mark left by the tide of the past, and awe-struck by the contrast between ROCOCO and 'GOTHIC Windsor' CHAIRS, between ADAM and VICTORIAN 'Elizabethan'.

It remains only to repeat the thought I offered in the first book about collecting. If you want your purchases to give you lasting satisfaction, to increase in value and to be a source of later pride, think of none of these things when you are buying, but only of your pleasure in the things themselves. But make it an *informed* pleasure.

JOHN BEDFORD

Adam

Collectors of jasper ware and black basaltes, made by Wedgwood and others towards the end of the eighteenth century, will already have a good idea of what is known as the Adam, or Neo-classical style. Put your Wedgwood urn or vase, with its classical reliefs, festoons, square pedestals and restrained curves, against a typical bit of ROCOCO whimsy – say a Louis XV ormolu clock – and you will see exactly what happened about the year 1760, when Robert Adam (1728–1792) and his brothers introduced the style here.

We talk of Adam fireplaces and ceilings rather than furniture, for though Adam designed furniture for the houses he built, it was very grand stuff for the grandees of the day: in furniture he set the mood for the simpler lines of Hepplewhite and Sheraton,

Adam sidetable, wine cooler, urn pedestals, vase and candlesticks

Late-18th-century silver epergne (Adam)

as opposed to the richer curves of Chippendale.
Adam fireplaces and doorways, even staircases, do
sometimes appear in the shops: I saw at a sale recently
a pinewood chimneypiece with all the usual Adam
trimmings – classical lamps, interleaved chains of
husks and ribbons, acanthus leaf corbals surmounted
by urns – and it made eighty pounds. But if you are
seriously looking for these items to restore a late
Georgian house you ought perhaps to go to somebody
like Bert Crowther of Isleworth, who collects them
from broken-up mansions vacated by broken-down
owners.

You can buy a piece of Adam fairly cheaply by
looking for one of the wooden urns in our sketch.
They were used either for storing cutlery or as cis-
terns for the washing-up water; there is often a metal
receptacle in the base for washing the silver in – and
also, it is said, for other uses arising out of the fact
that gentlemen dined late and the other offices were
a long way from the dining-room.

If Adam banished ROCOCO and BAROQUE, what, in
the end, happened to Adam? As usual, the classical
craze went too far: instead of using it as an inspiration,
the designers, for example, took great undigested
lumps of classical architecture, like temple façades and

columns, and stuck them on to bookcases and sideboards; they also dragged in Egyptian and other
oriental motifs, apparently derived from Napoleon's
cavorting around the Levant. Thus, REGENCY (one
is more polite about it under its own head).

19th-century teapot with classical motif

Adams

One of the pleasant things about potters is the way
they go on existing: sometimes for several hundred
years. This means that you can have fun looking at
their current products as well as their antique ones:
and, considering the pleasure given us by the old
wares, I hope my readers are sometimes decent enough
to buy a plate or two of the new, and thus keep the
potters happy and prosperous. (I remember getting a
rather reproachful look at Worcester once when I
suggested that mid-Victorian painted and gilt plates
could sometimes be bought more cheaply than the
current production.)

Adams is a name which has been connected with potting in Staffordshire since Elizabethan days, and probably before. Today, in their showroom, you can see not only reproductions of some of their own earlier designs – notably for the American market – but, what is more interesting, adaptations of designs in a modern idiom. It can be fun to put these alongside their predecessors.

Adams were early in the field with Staffordshire Printed Earthenware (*v. Looking in Junk Shops*), using an attractive and distinctive cobalt blue: and if all those printed with American views have long since disappeared, so too have most of the English views, especially those of places around London. In their borders, it may help to remember, they especially favoured bluebells.

But the various branches of the family have also had a hand in other wares of renown. Their jasper ware was more violet than Wedgwood's, and the reliefs freer in treatment; their black basaltes are worth looking for, and so is a fine caneware with coloured reliefs. Similar stoneware jugs to those made by Turner are sometimes found with the name impressed on the bottom and also in silver mounts: there are also some very attractive unglazed teapots faintly reminiscent of Castleford, with reliefs and sliding lids. Adams 'granite' ware is hard to find, being made for hard use rather than the cabinet.

Argyles

A device for insuring that dukes obtain their gravy hot and free from fatty scum. The invention of a Duke of Argyll, who had long suffered from the distances between kitchen and dining-room at Inveraray, it consists of a metal pot with a hollow chamber which

Late-18th-century silver argyle

can be filled with hot water. The spout for the gravy generally starts at the foot of the pot and comes up level with the top. Those in silver and Sheffield plate are as expensive as other articles in these materials, but there are occasionally to be found examples in ELECTRO-PLATE, of the 1850's and 1860's.

Art nouveau inkwell

Art Nouveau

Collectors are beginning to look more sympathetically at things in the Art Nouveau style of the period 1890–1910.

Up till now we have been rather rude about its 'sagging curves' and its 'boneless wonders': but I notice that a more recent writer has likened its typical lines to that of 'the lengthening spiral of cigarette smoke'. In England it is seen in glass, in pottery – particularly Royal LANCASTRIAN and Doulton – in metal orna-

Art nouveau chair

ments, in hand-fashioned jewellery, in book illustrations, in household furniture, fabrics, and light fittings. In all these departments there are interesting things to be got, still comfortably disregarded by the smart ones. I particularly like the vases, centre-pieces and inkwells in moulded and cast pewter, some of the 'majolica' vases with raised decoration, the lustre pots already mentioned and some fine needlework screens: the furniture is perhaps not easily assimilable in anything but traditional rooms.

Some hold that these long curves and writhing asymmetric shapes mark the first original VICTORIAN STYLE: others father it on a mixture of JAPANESQUE, Celtic art and William Morris's 'Arts and Crafts Movement'. In fact there is very little of it in the work of Morris and his followers; it would be truer to say that they cleared away the clutter of Victorian revivals and adaptations, thus creating a vacuum for the 'New Art'. This they did in Europe no less than here.

The style gets its name from a shop called 'L'Art Nouveau', which was opened in Paris in 1895 by a German art dealer called Samuel Bing: but in Germany it is called 'Jugendstil', after an art magazine called *Jugend* ('Youth'). In Italy it gets the name Stile Liberty, after the shop in Regent Street, which – up to date then as always – sold furnishings suited to it.

Astbury-Whieldon

This name is sometimes applied to a class of early Staffordshire pottery which is more usually associated with Thomas Whieldon than with the shadowy John Astbury: so the subject is dealt with under WHIELDON.

Ball-in-a-Ball

How on earth, you ask, can anyone put a carved ivory ball inside another carved ivory ball which is inside yet another carved ivory ball . . . and so on, sometimes up to twenty of them diminishing in size and all capable of being moved around in their prisons?

These objects, often beautifully carved, have a long history, and are still being made in the East. Making them, although very laborious, is not all that difficult. The carver takes a solid block of ivory and shapes it into a sphere. Then he drills holes at intervals around it down to a certain depth, cuts away with a side cutting tool until he has released one of the balls, then cuts through another layer in the same way, all the time working his carving into the hollow spheres. I believe they actually start with the smallest ball first.

The ball-in-a-ball, sometimes called Devil's ball, was a popular feature of the CHESSMEN from Canton and other Eastern centres.

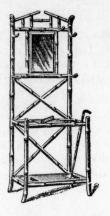

Bamboo hall stand and pot stand

Bamboo

Nobody can poke about for long in old furniture stores without coming across specimens of the bamboo furniture of which the Victorians were so fond around the time of the Jubilees. For such apparently tender stuff it is surprising how well it has hung together. Obviously inspired by that late VICTORIAN STYLE which one might call JAPANESQUE, the bamboo was usually combined with other canes, wicker or dried grasses: it took the form of high overmantels fitted with many small shelves and mirrors; of hat and umbrella stands and other sorts of hall furniture; of many sorts of little tables, of music canterburies, trays, picture frames, brackets, lamp-standards, even Chesterfield SETTEES upholstered – just to mix things up – with 'Djijm Kelims'.

None of this furniture was ever, it seems, made in Japan: and the London suppliers would not only furnish out a whole room for you, but would make the pieces especially to fit your circumstances: they would even mount your own embroidery on bamboo screens.

Being so fragile, most of the pieces one sees are somewhat battered, and would, I suppose, be expensive to repair by anything except amateur labour. But if people should decide they want it – and one has seen far less likely revivals – I daresay this will be remedied in the twinkling of a dealer's eye.

While on this subject one ought to mention another sort of Bamboo Ware which dates from RE-GENCY days. This was really a piece of Chinoiserie rather than Japanesquerie, whereby bamboo was imitated in beechwood by turning the legs with the typical notches of the bamboo cane (see page 53 below). Some of the CHAIRS with cane panel backs having medallions painted in the centre are for me charming compromises between hard-to-live-up-to Hepplewhite and those chummy affairs with straw seats and spindle backs which you and I, had we lived then, might have had in our parlour.

Baroque gilt pedestal

Baroque

This is another of those words which get tossed around by superior people like the interior decorator or the guide in a stately home. Actually, it describes something which you must know by sight already, so it might be amusing to toss it back perhaps with some trimmings of your own. If you happen to be a native of Britain, Baroque will have caught your eye mainly in the form of full rich curves and mouldings of furniture of the Restoration, WILLIAM AND MARY, and early QUEEN ANNE periods. Everything about it is rich, flowing, elaborate and very, very grand. Chippendale liked these curves, but used them with English restraint.

Baroque has sometimes been called the male version of ROCOCO: another way of putting it might be to say that ROCOCO is Baroque being frivolous.

Bartolozzi print

Bartolozzi

Time does not dim enthusiasm for the world shown in the stipple engravings of Francesco Bartolozzi (1728–1813), a world of lovely ladies, elegant gentlemen and adorable children, of delicious shepherdesses and their manly swains, of classical allegories ('Cupid Bound by Nymphs'), of sweet sentiments and lofty thoughts.

Bartolozzi engravings after painters like Cipriani, Angelica KAUFFMANN, and others, are to be taken as charming decorations rather than serious art. But to make sure that you have a print which is 'right' is a very serious business indeed, and full of hazards. In this fore-runner of the half-tone block, the design is lightly etched in with a series of dots, and the colours used are on one plate instead of several different ones. It was an enormously complicated business. The engraver had first to work in the dominant tint, then leave just enough in the bitten-out 'dots' to take other colours. For the flesh tints he even had to warm the plate to precisely the right temperature.

These technical considerations are offered to show how rare and precious a thing an early Bartolozzi print must be. Without the coloured 'dots' – which you can easily see – you have merely a modern reproduction in some other process: even with them you are still not out of the wood, for although there are many a thousand of genuine stipple engravings, most of these are not a patch on the fine 'early states' which make the big prices.

So, if you want a pretty picture with old-world charm, there are 'genuine' prints made in later times from the original plates, and there are reproductions of them, either as separate prints or in books, in every

sort of colour printing process known to man – and
will be so long as people want them. But if you want
the pleasure of discovering the real qualities of this
most difficult art, go to a recognised print dealer and
tell him how much you have to spend.

Baxter Prints

Fitting enough that George Baxter (1804–1867) should
follow Francesco BARTOLOZZI, for his colour prints,
as brilliant as the oil paintings they did duty for in
the mid-Victorian home, represent the next big advance in this field. Working on an aquatint or mezzotint foundation, the colour was provided by as many
as twenty blocks, each with a different tint. The
process is not very different from that used on potlids
by Pratts of Fenton and others (*v. Looking in Junk
Shops*); both called for high qualities of craftsmanship
in getting correct register and tints.

Baxter's best work, which is of superb quality, is,
and has for long been, scarce and pricey. There are
his famous missionary prints, like 'Descent from the
Cross' and 'The Ascension', the enormously popular
flower pictures following the Dutch masters, landscapes, dancing girls, charmingly sentimental scenes
and elaborate groups on public occasions. 'Baxtero-
types' in monochrome are often to be seen, popular
ones being the pair entitled 'The Crucifixion' and
'The Holy Family'. There was also a set of these
taken from the Raphael Cartoons.

Apart from the full-scale reprints and book illustrations, Baxter also printed a range of very collectable
smaller items. There were small prints for pocket
books and Sunday School cards, printed notepaper,
pieces for scrapbooks, miniature pictures for the tops
of needleboxes. Collectors especially like the delightful

little 'Fairies' set, and there were also series showing the Royal Family in its various official and private activities, scriptural stories, dancing and 'harem' scenes.

Baxter prints, if they were made in his workshop, usually bear his name, and their date can be found by reference to the address; but of course there are modern forgeries, particularly of the mounts. After 1849, he sold licences for his process to other printers like Le Blond, Joseph Mansell, William Dickes, J. M. Kronheim; and the work of these men also has its ardent collectors. Le Blond 'ovals', pleasant little pictures of village life, are especially attractive.

Victorian bead bag

Beadwork

Beads and bugles (these latter are the long tube-shaped ones) have been made of glass in imitation of JEWELLERY since the times of Ancient Egypt, and have been in demand for rosaries and necklaces ever since.

They have also been worked into all manner of embroidery. Still to be found very reasonably priced nowadays are all those little items like bracelets, hair ornaments, brooches and other costume JEWELLERY; also handbags, table mats, work tidies and boxes, stocking or miser purses, book covers, baskets, spectacle covers, etc. Beads have also been worked on chair seats and covers, screens, footstool covers, tea cosies and a host of similar domestic items. Beadwork pictures, in point of time, followed STUMPWORK pictures and chiefly show landscapes and animal subjects, worked on a silk or satin foundation: these are getting pricey, if in good condition.

Some beads are so tiny that the hole is too small for the needle; these were sewn on with a special thread. There are also pieces decorated with the eighteenth- and early nineteenth-century cut-steel beads mentioned under JEWELLERY. Gilt metal was also used.

One of the nice things about collecting old beadwork is that if you are a needlewoman and take the trouble to learn old methods and styles, damaged pieces can be repaired at home. You could also go a little further and sell it back to the trade: they couldn't possibly get the work done any more cheaply than you do it yourself.

Bear Jugs

We no longer bait bears, but we can still buy bear-baiting jugs. They take the form of a bear sitting up

Bear jug

on its haunches, hugging a dog to its furry breast. Attendants took them round, filled with ale, at bear-baiting tourneys.

Great rarities now, and only to be found in the big sales, are the ones in early Staffordshire salt-glaze, and so also are those in NOTTINGHAM WARE covered with clay chips to imitate the animal's fur. But there are rather later ones in earthenware covered with a brown slip, and there are also quite a few in nine-teenth-century BROWNWARE. Bear-baiting would have died out long before they were made so they must have been among the items made at that time to entrap collectors of the eighteenth-century ware.

Some bear jugs were adapted to current affairs of the time: one well-known model dates itself pretty closely by showing, instead of a dog, a figure of Napoleon being crushed by a Russian bear. There is also another quite different race where the dog is actually attached to the bear's stomach and becomes a spout.

Bed Steps

When beds stood higher off the floor than they do now – and if the statisticians are right we were all shorter then – it was handy to have something to help you climb up into your fragrant sheets, nicely

Early 19th-century bed steps

aired with the warming pan. For this job came the set of bed steps – which nowadays one finds handier for getting books off the top shelf in a library. Some models include a night commode.

Bellarmines

These are the familiar globular bottles in brown mottled stoneware, with long narrow necks, the front marked with a mask of a bearded man. They originally came to this country, along with Rhenish wine and RUMMERS, under the name of 'Cologne Ware', but they were also made by the English potters of the seventeenth century like Dwight of Fulham.

They have for long borne the name of Cardinal Roberto Bellarmino, said to have been a rigorous persecutor of Protestants in the Low Countries during the Spanish occupation in the seventeenth century. A 'gallonier' contained a gallon, a 'pottle pot' two quarts, a 'pot' a quart, and a 'little pot' a pint.

Bellarmine

How unpleasant or pleasant a person Bellarmino might have been you can discover for yourself by reading the biography published recently. Actually, the jugs named after him were made long before he was born; they seem, in fact, to have descended from similar bottles bearing the masks of lions and other animals. So here, it seems, we have the case of a character getting his name attached to something which already existed (like the BLIND EARL pattern).

An even odder fact about them is that they have been found buried in ditches containing nasty and spooky things like cloth hearts pierced with pins, fingernail parings, human hair and other appurtenances of witchcraft.

Benares Ware

What has become, one wonders, of all the old Benares brassware which Anglo-Indians or globe-trotting tourists once brought home? One sees a little of it about, but not nearly as much as might have been expected.

Benares brass tray with scalloped edge

Finest of all, naturally, is the early ware made before the setting in of self-conscious catering for the tourist trade. It gave us, in a metal as brilliant as gold, cauldrons, pots, bowls, shovels, snuffers, salvers, betel-nut holders, goblets, flower holders, all with beautifully chased and EMBOSSED designs, often using a 'frosted' background effect. But the later work is much less brilliant and suffers from overcrowded and monotonous ornamentation.

This is as good a place as any, however, to call attention to the wonderful range of shapes in Indian metalwork vessels. There is the long-necked *Surahi*, or water vessel, with a stopper (see page 26); also the *Lota*, a slightly flattened globular drinking vessel with a turned-out rim – a shape made continuously for two thousand years. No room to illustrate or describe the many others, such as the *Galubdani*, for sprinkling water at religious ceremonies, the *Bandan*, a case for holding betel-nut leaves, the *Bivala*, a metal cup, and the bell-shaped *Hukka* (or Hookah) bowl.

Bewick

Books illustrated by Thomas Bewick (1753–1828) have so long been choice collecting that you may wonder

Bewick engraving

to find him mentioned here. But even if you cannot afford a copy of his *Quadrupeds* (1790) and *British Birds* (1797–1804) or his *Select Fables* (1818), there are plenty of books about which reproduce these marvellous little pictures and vignettes. There are biographies of Bewick which show them and can be bought for very little: and quite recently I found a copy of Robert Bloomfield's long poem *The Farmer's Boy*, which, although not a first edition, has Bewick's engravings – it cost me three shillings.

What is there about Bewick's little pictures that his work should be so admired? Well, even if we are not all of us countrymen, few are more than a generation or two away from the countryside: and Bewick's wonderful eye for animals and birds and the minutiae of the rural scene has profoundly satisfied readers for over a century. But what many find the most entrancing part of his work are the little vignettes he used for chapter endings. His idea of doing these, he claimed, was to make these rather solid books of natural history more entertaining for young readers: but while many do show gay and cheerful country scenes, others point the grimmest sort of morals – there is even one of a suicide. The truth seems to be that he simply enjoyed doing them.

Technically, Bewick's work is important because he managed to reproduce in wood the tonal effect of engravings on copper. He did this by reversing the old woodcut process. Instead of cutting away the whites to leave a black line, he cut the design itself in his famous 'white line'. He also lowered the surface of the block to give greys.

Bewick left a school of followers like William Harvey, Charlton Nesbit and Luke Clennell, whose work I have in a copy (three shillings) of Northcote's *Fables*.

But they none of them have quite the touch or the technique of the master: this, to my mind, is shown more effectively in the work of the later wood-engravers.

But don't let's get too technical about Bewick. Buy the best examples of his work you can and just enjoy the way they show the very spirit of the birds and animals, the country people and the scenes among which it was possible for a craftsman to live in those days.

Bidri Work

Not so frequently found as it once was, like old BENARES ware, is this handsome variety of DAMASCENING

Bidri ware surahi

made in Bidar, Hyderabad, and other centres. Ash trays, hukka bowls, spittoons, cups, plates, tumblers, flower vases, cake stands, small boxes and even teapots are found in this fine 'silver and black' ware, as well as the set of household utensils customary as a bride's dowry in Hyderabad.

The alloy is similar to pewter, being of zinc, copper, lead and tin. After inlaying the decorative work in silver, the piece is turned jet black by a chemical solution, after which the silver is polished so that it shows up against the black background.

Anyone having fine pieces of old Bidri work, with fine floral decoration, is to be envied, for this kind of craftsmanship even if it continues, will become more expensive to find as time goes on.

Billingsley

One sees so many flowers on junk-shop pieces which owe at least something to William Billingsley (1760–1828), perhaps the most famous and at the same time the most unfortunate of china painters, that one ought to tarry a moment with him.

Billingsley started his career at Derby in 1774, and founded a style of china painting which was much more naturalistic than the rather formal method inherited from the eighteenth century. His flowers had much greater depth, and he 'wiped out' his highlights, as some oil-painters do.

Had he stuck to painting, Billingsley might have been a prosperous and highly successful man, but he thought of himself primarily as an 'arcanist' in pottery, i.e. one who possesses secret formulae for making it. Unfortunately the porcelain he made at Pinxton, Nantgarw, Swansea and elsewhere, though of exquisite quality, was so wasteful in production that it involved him in endless heartbreaks, distress and debt; to which misfortunes were added the deaths, within a few weeks of each other, of his two cherished daughters, who travelled around and worked with him.

Eventually Billingsley found a safe harbour as a painter with Rose of Coalport, and died in 1828. But there is always a 'Billingsley Rose' in production somewhere.

Bird Cages

When the Victorians sang their heart-rending ditties – as folks still do in the pubs off the Mile End Road – about being only a bird in a gilded cage, they were doubtless thinking of the magnificent brass affairs which stood on their parlour tables.

From a shop catalogue of the day one sees that they had the offer of plenty of them; sometimes small and round, sometimes large and square or octagonal: either way they had those peculiarly 'different' lines which the modern manufacturer is too efficient to be

'Crystal Palace' bird cage

able to produce – and which for us constitutes the period charm. The cages, with their gilding, their cut ruby glass surrounds, their wire trapezes, their little golden bells, are much admired and desired today: you can, if you look hard, find them domed, 'wagon-shaped' and sometimes even grander – like the 'Crystal Palace Aviary', in polished mahogany and tinned wire offered by Harrods in 1900 for 38s. 6d.

For those who like to be sure that their bird will sing there are cages already supplied with a bird whose native woodnotes wild come from a small reed organ, carefully hidden away below decks: the songster, perched upon a wire bush above the papier mâché floor, seems to be pouring out his profuse strains of unpremeditated art entirely on his Tod Malone. Many ingenious cages of this sort survive, and their number has been increased with the help of modern manufacturers. The decorators love them, especially if they have clients for VICTORIAN LOUIS décor of whatever number. Further notions along these lines are indicated under MUSICAL BOXES.

Blackamoor

Always price one of these small negro figures, for they fetch a good sum in the big salerooms; if they have been knocked about, they can be restored.

A negro boy, perhaps in Oriental costume or livery, was a necessary part of a fashionable lady's house in the eighteenth century; so in default of a live one they appeared as table bases or as free standing figures about three feet high, presumably for the same purposes as DUMMY BOARD FIGURES.

Regency 'blackamoor' pedestal

Sometimes they hold candelabra, or act as small occasional tables. They were popular again in Victorian days, with girls as well as boys.

Black Jacks
Although we still find leather the finest stuff for keeping our feet dry-shod, we do not at first think of it as a container for liquids. We did not always think so. A seventeenth-century rhyme scorns the tankard, flagon, bottle or jug, saying:

> *For when they are broken or full of cracks,*
> *Then must one fly to the brave black jacks.*

Black Jacks were large leather jugs, sometimes over eighteen inches in height, with loop handles and usually a metal rim, and they often come up at clear-

ance sales of farms, old houses, and inns. There were
also bottles (the 'lether bottel' of the song), and pots
or tankards with silver rims, sometimes mounted with
crests or initials of the former owners.

I have a 'black jack' of my own which is modern,
and not really of leather, but of some form of plastic.
I found it among several dozen others in a lot of sur-
plus army stores, and it was evidently used for handling acid. Still, it is big, jug-shaped, nice to handle,
cost me half-a-crown, and you should see what it
does for marigolds.

Blind Earl

A famous pattern at Worcester, with large impressed
or painted leaves, said to have been designed for a
blind Earl of Coventry, so that he could feel the
pattern.

It was actually in existence before the Earl went
blind but it seems to have been the practice at Worcester to name existing patterns after patrons who
favoured them. Worcester still uses the pattern today.

Blue John

This famous Derbyshire stone, a type of fluorspar,
fetches high prices nowadays – why, I find it rather
difficult to guess. True, the material itself is a pleasant
enough thing – gold or honey-coloured stone with
darker, sometimes purple markings – but the ornaments made of it are usually in the most unadventurous
type of NEO-CLASSICAL shapes.

There are egg-shaped things with square white
marble bases, chalices with cup-spaded bowls, *tazzi*
(if that is the plural of *tazza*) large vases, bell-shaped
urns, obelisks, and also smaller items like scent bottles
with gilt stoppers, pendants, cylindrical vesta boxes.

I really cannot value these things at the twenty to forty pounds or more that ardent collectors are prepared to pay for them: and this opinion, for what it is worth, goes also for those similar wares in Cornish Serpentine and other English native stones. One feels that we should have imported some French or Italian workers, as they did at Nailsea.

Bonbonnière

Bonbonnières

A bonbonnière is a little box, usually in enamels or precious metals, in which are carried bonbons, cachous or comfits. You used one when you lived in the eighteenth century to give fragrance to the breath or perhaps simply as something to offer round, like a cigarette case.

The box was often round: those in Battersea or Bilston enamel (*v. Looking in Junk Shops*) are well beyond our reach, but there are tortoiseshell ones, sometimes ornamented with PIQUÉ work. They also come in porcelain and china, and in Wedgwood jasper ware.

What were these 'comfits'? Apparently such delicacies as coriander and caraway seeds, cloves and other herbs, sugared and spiced and coloured up attractively. Sometimes, instead of being put in a box, they would be in a tiny tray or basket held out to you by porcelain or china children or shepherdesses.

Bone Carving

If we like intricate, and sometimes quite beautiful, carving we must not overlook bone, that humble relative of ivory – which is only elephant bone anyway, although of course with quite special qualities of hardness, translucency when thin, of soft tones and of taking a beautiful polish.

But carvers used bone usually because it was all they had to hand; and most of what we see is the work of prisoners-of-war making use of what was left of their frugal meals, to be sold to visitors for the means of buying tobacco. Ships equipped with standing and running rigging are perhaps the best-known examples of this work, and when they turn up either in general shops or in specialist places like the Parker Gallery, they are no longer to be had for ha'pence.

However, there are many other sorts of things. I saw a beautiful games box recently, its sides inset with pictures of coloured landscapes and flowers, these pictures being behind glass. There were dominoes, of course, but also to my surprise a complete set of cards made of flat pieces of bone. Another item at a sale was a working model of a guillotine, with soldiers standing over the victim, whose head was cut off neatly by a tortoiseshell blade. More cheerful was a working SPINNING WHEEL, with two women working it.

I notice that the seaside gift shops have suddenly burgeoned forth with thin bone carvings of some delicacy, but showing signs of mechanical work. Should one suspect Hong Kong, where the BALL-IN-A-BALL is still made?

18th-century satinwood bonheur du jour

Bonheur du Jour
How pleasant to have an elegant little writing desk
which wishes you 'the happiness of the morning'!

That is the name of the piece shown here, originally made in the France of LOUIS XV or XVI for ladies
to sit at and write all those letters and diaries. Sometimes there were mirrors in the side panels, as an
aid to concentration.

Booth's Silicon China
Anyone who is fond of the shapes and styles of early
Worcester, and does not mind having them in fine
Victorian earthenware rather than eighteenth-century soft-paste porcelain (v. *Looking in Junk Shops*),
might look out for pieces of Booth's Silicon China,
made at Tunstall from about 1900.

Booth's 'Worcester'

Here are the perforated baskets and plates, the flower vases, tea wares, leaf-shaped dishes, coffee pots, and the rest, with rose peonies, exotic birds in gay plumage and all the other felicities of Dr Wall's reign on Severnside. Although one of the marks bears the date 1750, this is (one hopes) intended to mark the pattern rather than the date of manufacture, but in any case the firm's name is there as well – when it hasn't been removed by some enterprising dealer.

Boots and Shoes

I know a lady who has a most wonderful collection of boots and shoes – not real ones but miniatures of glass, china, earthenware, silver, pewter, wood and brass. Except for the porcelain ones they are not very expensive items, for most of them were made as novelties to be sold very cheaply, or perhaps as containers for perfume, etc.

China and glass shoes

What I find interesting about them, however, is the different styles and types of footwear they show to have been used over the past couple of centuries – some of them so charming that one wonders they have never been revived. Ladies' high-laced boots of about the mid-nineteenth century show the tooling in the leather: little slippers in Spatter Glass have trimming in clear glass, slippers in opaque glass are often cased with coloured glass to show patterns sewn on. There are babies' bootees, men's jackboots, moccasins, dancing shoes, shoes with skates. As to use, apart from those already mentioned, you can find little boots in the shape of RUMMERS – very popular in hunt clubs for drinking toasts 'in a lady's shoe'. There are shoe and boot ink bottles, thimble holders, match containers, ash trays, salt and pepper pots, Vaseline jars, flower-holders, spoon-holders, lamps, wall-pockets. Some of these, though originally sold as containers of something, often carried the something in a bottle which fitted into the shoe or boot, but which has now been lost. Look for the Registry Mark on some of these glass slippers: this will lead you to date and manufacturer (v. *Looking in Junk Shops*).

Still in the shops today, of course, are the modern Dutch 'delftware' bottles, and if you are a real collector you won't despise these: what you throw away today your grandchildren will eagerly collect tomorrow. Where, for example, are all those lovely small shoe bottles and boxes in Victorian bone china, with beautiful hand painting, made for *your* grandmother?

But china and glass is only the beginning of your shoe shop. Pewter and silver ones, with pincushions in the top, are still about; there are enamel boxes and bottles too.

This is another of those quests which can be pursued on your foreign holiday, for in other countries you will find a whole lot more styles. Look out for Customs duty: if you can't prove a thing is a century old you may have to pay a little on the value of the shoe's material.

Bridge Jugs
A term sometimes used to describe the transfer printed jugs with views of WEARMOUTH BRIDGE, which most people know as SUNDERLAND BRIDGE, q.v.

Britannia Metal
Now that both silver and Sheffield plate are very much a rich man's quarry, quite a few of us have been looking at what is to be found in Britannia metal. One of the discoveries one makes is that table wares made in it have some extraordinarily fine and simple shapes; another that its sheen, rather like that of pewter, can appeal to one as much as silver – unless the silver is very old.

Pewter has been mentioned above, and when you pick up a piece of Britannia metal and ask the dealer what it is, nine times out of ten he will tell you it *is* pewter. He is very nearly right, for it is an alloy of tin, antimony and copper, differing only from the usual pewter alloy by having no lead in it. The dealer's criterion is that he gets about the same

Britannia metal teapot

price for both as scrap – about five shillings an ounce.

Britannia metal emerged in the late eighteenth century when John Vickers started using an early version of it under the name of Vickers Metal, or White Metal, for pieces in the styles of Sheffield plate. Up to the time of the invention of ELECTRO-PLATE, Britannia metal appeared wearing its own skin, which was a passable imitation of silver; but time took off this sheen and the pieces would settle down to the quiet grey glow of pewter. This did not suit the Victorians very well, for they wanted their guests to think they really could afford silver, so upon the invention of ELECTRO-PLATE in the eighteen-forties, many articles of Britannia metal were put through this process and given a coating of silver. They can be spotted by the letters EPBM on the base (electro-plated Britannia metal). But an enormous amount of the metal must have been sent out just as it was, for this is what one finds nowadays. On the other hand, much of it, if not sold as scrap, is being sent by dealers to the platers,

where after acquiring a hard cold silver coat it goes
to the flashy shops in seaside resorts. The word
Sheffield, a number, and perhaps the name of a
maker like Dixon's, lead some people wrongly to infer
that it may be Sheffield plate.

British Plate

This was a development of Sheffield Plate (*v. Looking
in Junk Shops*). It had the advantage that its core
was not of copper, but of a silver-coloured alloy
which did not show through when the silver coating
became worn. Its manufacturers often hopefully
stamped it with devices intended to pass as silver
hallmarks.

The alloy was known as GERMAN SILVER from its
place of origin, and it included copper, zinc and
nickel. Articles made of British Plate followed the
styles of Sheffield Plate, but were sometimes given
solid silver mounts. Occasionally pieces may be found
which bear the letters EPGS (electro-plated GERMAN
SILVER) instead of the more usual EPNS (electro-
plated nickel silver) the alloy used in ELECTRO-PLATE –
which eventually superseded it.

Brownware

Collectors with a taste for the unusual rather than the
conventionally pretty have long been putting together
the many different sorts of things made in what seems
nowadays to be generally known as Brownware, or
saltglazed brown stoneware.

You may recognize it in the famous HUNTING JUGS
and mugs, puzzle jugs with their baffling spouts and
holes, cylindrical jugs called 'canettes', two-handled
POSSET POTS and LOVING CUPS, candlesticks, tea kettles,
tobacco jars, decorative twisted tobacco pipes after

Brownware mug

the manner of Nailsea, BEAR JUGS, Toby jugs, 'wind-mill' jugs, but most of all perhaps that astonishing range of spirit bottles described in *Looking in Junk Shops*.

In buff, brown or deep chocolate stoneware of an immense hardness, with carvings or impressed designs, and showing scarcely any marks of time however old they are, these pieces were so popular with collectors in late Victorian days that the potters of the day obliged with replicas of what they had made a hundred years before. Today, therefore, in the absence of a mark, it is often very difficult to trace a piece not only to a maker but to a century. However, no true collector has ever been put off by a consideration like this, so here is the quarry for those who like detective work, as well as the pleasure of handling fine masculine wares of a type whose ancestry goes back through very many centuries and civilisations.

Among the marks you do find on these pieces are those of potters in the Chesterfield district, especially Brampton, e.g., names like Knowles, Oldfield, Briddon, Bourne.

Burmantofts

This Leeds factory was once famous for its tiles, FLOWER POTS AND PEDESTALS in Victorian 'faience', and also for 'art' pottery in the fine glazes worked out in the eighties and nineties.

The shapes of the pottery may seem a little bizarre to our eyes, but the FLAMBÉ, SANG DE BOEUF, and other glazes are magnificent.

There was an amusing sideline in some grotesque but well-modelled figures, particularly a toad which could be either a vase or a money box.

Calabash

An explanation of this long-lived shape is offered under GOURD.

Cameo Glass

Vases, bottles and other pieces in carved cameo glass, with figures and other designs standing out in relief in opal glass on a darker ground, sometimes appear in the salerooms, and when they do they fetch very good prices. So if you see a good one going cheaply, snap it up.

They derive from a sharp break with the English tradition of cut glass pioneered by John Northwood, of Wordsley, in the famous glassmaking district of Stourbridge. Northwood's original work, in which he laboured for years over such tours-de-force as a replica of the Portland Vase, is rare and priceless, and so also is the handiwork of such disciples of his as the Woodall brothers.

Cameo glass vase with foliate design

But a later development of this was 'commercial' cameo, which eliminated a great deal of the work of carving the relief figures, and so made it possible to market the ware at reasonable – though by no means low – prices.

The engraving wheel was brought into use to help out with the carving, and the opal glass was 'cased' to the body more thinly, thus leaving less to cut away and reveal the coloured body beneath.

Many of the pieces found nowadays have the classical themes of the times, but personally I prefer the very fine patterns of leaves and flowers, the sort of designs in which the latish Victorians really excelled. But, as I said at the beginning, you will have to be eagle-eyed to get even 'commercial' cameo very cheaply.

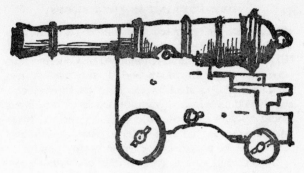

Early 19th-century ship's cannon

Cannon

If you like firing salutes when friends come to tea it will not cost you a great deal to buy the cannon, nor take you very long to find it.

'To make the mixture fit for great guns, mortars and other pieces of artillery,' says a gentleman named Malachyn Postlethwayt, writing in the year 1751, 'the best and softest tin of Cornwall is a necessary ingredient skilfully applied. There must be six, seven or eight pounds of it to the 100 weight of red copper.' As Britain was laying the foundations of an empire about that time, this recipe seems to have been a reasonably successful one: perhaps we should have stuck to it.

Most difficult sort of cannon to find, naturally, are those which have survived some historic action and also escaped melting down into souvenirs. But there are plenty of nameless ones which have probably done just as well in their quiet (if that is the word) way. I saw several cast-iron ones sold last year for no very great sum, considering. A couple of them, one of about 1820, the other ten years older – it could have been at Waterloo – thirty-one-inch and forty-one-inch barrel length respectively, mounted on contemporary carriages, went for thirty pounds the two. A trio, each with the crest of an elephant on the breech – they would have looked grand drawn up in line abreast facing up your drive – made the same money. Brass-barrelled signal cannon signed with the makers' initials can be picked up for ten to twenty pounds.

Even if your garden consists only of a window box you can have your artillery. Miniature cannon, either of cast iron or engraved brass, say eight to fifteen inches long, can be found at about half the above prices.

Cane Ware

Here is a kind of pottery which I think we might look at more closely. As with many another sort, a single piece may not look very much, but a lot can look very interesting, and in fact show a surprising diversity.

What I am talking about is a buff, or tan-coloured, dry (unglazed) stoneware, often enamelled in blue

Cane Ware bulb-pot

and colours. Outstanding pieces are the well-known piecrust dishes made in the form of a game pie and intended to act as a substitute for the pastry which shortage of flour denied our citizens during the Napoleonic wars. Another well-known one is the BAMBOO style bulb pot which one often sees. These were quite a happy invention, for each stick of 'bamboo' around the pot had a hole at its end for an individual flower, as well as the central holes for the bulbs.

But these are merely the show-offs of the family: I prefer all those nice little teapots and sugar bowls with reliefs of cherubs and other subjects, and sparingly lined in blue or green. Wedgwood was a pioneer in Cane Ware as well as in most other fields, but it was also made by Turner of Lane End, Mayer and others.

Caudle Cups

Among the odder drinks favoured by our ancestors was caudle, a sort of custard made of oatmeal or biscuit mixed with hot wine or beer, then spiced or sweetened. It was given to invalids, women in child-

Caudle cup

bed and anyone else who needed cossetting, also to those visiting them: at first in a covered cup with a spout (in fact, the POSSET POT, q.v.), and later in a two-handled cup with a saucer and cover, the imbiber using a spoon instead of, presumably, sucking the stuff through the spout.

Often mistaken for chocolate cups (which had only one handle), these caudle cups sometimes come in matching sets, and even EN SUITE with a tea and coffee set. Worcester made them, so did Chelsea, Derby, and Caughley.

They could, I suppose, be the ancestors of those covered 'cabinet cups' made for display by the Victorian factories in bone china.

Chairs

Here is where we have to take a very deep breath. Ever since Western man found he preferred to sit only halfway down to the ground, he has been making and buying these useful and sometimes decorative objects in an astonishing variety of styles and materials. Chairs wear out more quickly than other sorts of furniture, and so have to be replaced more often: it has consequently been easier to express in them the latest notion – original or stolen, felicitous or monstrous – of the furniture designer.

So when we look round even the junkiest of shops we can expect to find hints and echoes of practically every idea these men have ever had. Only the other day I saw a carved wooden X chair which had been chucked on the top of a sideboard and was awaiting a purchaser at three pounds. In other incarnations, such chairs have occupied proud places in Roman villas, ancient Egyptian temples, Italian palaces of the Renaissance, in the Tudor Court and Stuart Courts: at

Left: 'X', Dante or Savonarola; *Right:* 'Abbotsford'

various times they have also borne the name of *Dante*, *Savonarola*, and *Glastonbury* after their presumed users. They are to be seen in many a Victorian photograph album, and I suspect that most of the ones we see now came out of bankrupt Victorian photographers' studios.

It would be a lengthy and much too tedious job to try to get all these chairs into classifications, but there is one rough division which is worth making. This is a distinction between what one might call 'country kitchen' chairs and the rest. I do this partly because I like the first kind best, but also because, although you can mix a lot of different furniture, I don't think you would particularly want to mix these two very different sorts.

Right at the heart of the 'country kitchen' school, of course, is the Windsor, in all its many flowerings both in England and the United States – some say more skilfully in the former than in the latter. This has

Left: Ladder- or slat-back; *Right:* Spindle- or bobbin-back

already been covered in *Looking in Junk Shops*: but a distant cousin even older in origin, and lasting down to today, is the *Ladder-back,* or *Slat-back.* This usually has a rush seat, but as these wear out you may have to be content, like me, to buy one for eighteen shillings with a replacement of shaped plywood; however, there are still craftsmen in England who can give a chair another rush seat when it needs one. These chairs are known also in Normandy, finely carved, from the sixteenth century: perhaps they arrived in America via French Canada. As well as the plain slats there are those 'wave' cut (see above), popular in England and also New England: the 'salamander', more often seen in America; and the shape like an oiled and parted Edwardian moustache – which in the older English version is upside down, and was still being made by Ernest Gimson in 1910. It will be noted that the chair in the sketch has a shaped and a turned ball foot which tries to hint at the *cabriole*

Left: Mendlesham; *Right:* Winged rocker

effect more often found in the drawing-room.

Then we have the *Spindle-back*, or *Bobbin-back*, that most modestly gracious of chairs, used, one feels sure, by the sort of people who like nice things but are themselves much too nice to be able to afford extravagances. This goes back to Stuart times and forward to William Morris: but is suspected of a Scandinavian origin, and so far as the English version is concerned they are said to have come up the Severn with the Norse invaders of the north of England where (before sales and auctions scattered them all over the place) they were chiefly to be found. One variety, with the spindles grouped towards the centre rather than across the back, has been called a *Lancashire* chair. Whether spindled or laddered, they also have rush seats, and so enjoy that pleasant 'give' which is as comfortable as any upholstery and a fine tribute to the local craftsmen's skill.

Talking locally again, there are the *Mendlesham*, or

D

Left: West Country; *Right:* Country Chippendale

'*Dan Day*' chairs made at the Suffolk village and by the person named: usually of yew and fruit wood, they are a fairly close relative of the Windsor but adding nicely placed ball ornaments, a trick which Dan Day's son Richard is supposed to have learned while working for Sheraton. Similar chairs are said to have been made at Scole in Norfolk.

More primitive is the simple *West Country* chair, but it needs no very sharp eye to see its relationship not only with the chairs we have been discussing but also with the American *Carvers* and *Brewsters*.

More sophisticated is the whole range of chairs which have been called *Country Chippendale*. These are not really kitchen chairs: they were the middle-class approach to the fine furnishing of the gentry but nowadays they take their place in the kitchen along with all the other honest stuff.

To the wooden family also, but perhaps more often seen in the 'parlour' than the kitchen, belongs a late-

Left: Fireside; *Right:* Bentwood rocker

comer from Austria, the *Bentwood* chair. These were first shown in England at the Great Exhibition of 1851 by Michael Thonet, and they were not only a huge success for the next eighty years, but have given birth to descendants in 'modern' and also 'contemporary' furniture, especially from Sweden. Victorian bentwood could be bought for shillings until quite recently, and is not expensive now.

Last of our group from the stone-flagged floor, the low ceiling and the casement window comes the *Rocker*. This is a chair which the Americans have made more of than the English, having turned it into a national institution, their main types being the *Boston*, the *Sleepy Hollow*, and the *Lincoln*. Mr Dreppard (READING LIST) says that there are, first, rockers which have been converted – usually Windsor Slat-backs, Spindle-backs, and the rest, with iron or wooden bends attached to them; and second, the rockers built *as* rockers, with features ordinary chairs don't have.

Left: Hall chair; *Right:* Balloon back

The rocker shown, with wings against the draught, was used by John Wesley, and I have seen lots of Windsors here with 'carpet cutters' – many were made in the High Wycombe district. Nowadays we have got interested in rockers again, and they are being sold in England, not only in traditional styles and materials from Wycombe and Sweden, but also in the latest 'contemporary' manner with nylon-strung back, bent mahogany and ash. Doctors recommend them to ease the strain as the country goes steadily downhill: perhaps this is the era of the English rocker.

Moving out of the kitchen, through the green baize door and along the hall, the first thing we find is the *Hall* chair, the most universally uncomfortable thing ever offered for the human behind. They have been in existence since the eighteenth century, and were so designed, it is thought, (a) because anyone allowed to wait in the hall was expected to leave as soon as possible; (b) because he was probably wet with rain and

Left: Cockfighting (?); *Right:* Reading or library

mud and so might spoil an upholstered chair. Anyway, there they all are, mostly from Victorian halls, with hard wooden seats, scrolled and carved backs – exquisitely painful to lean against, and surely useable only as decoration.

Then there is the REGENCY version of BAMBOO, already mentioned under that head, wherein beechwood was turned to look like the Oriental wood. If we glance into the library or the gunroom we may be able to settle a longstanding controversy about the difference between a *Cockfighting* chair and a *Library* chair: in both the gentleman sat astride, but the one with the armrest would allow him to lean forward to watch the main more closely, while the one with the book rest would be handy for a book. Why should one sit astride to read in one's library? Possibly because one preferred to keep one's long-skirted coat-tails uncreased.

A much more thoughtful affair is the *Roundabout*, which has semi-circular arms, and the seat on the

skew so that there is one leg in front. These are sometimes called *Corner* chairs, because they fit well in
corners, and also *Writing* chairs because you can pull
them up to a desk or table. These can be found in the
'country kitchen' family as well.

If we are going in for stateliness, there is first the
Dante or *X* chair already mentioned, and then the
Abbotsford. As its name suggests, this is a legacy of
Sir Walter Scott's historical romances in which JACO-
BEAN has got itself gloriously mixed up with GOTHIC in
a pastiche of a chair popular in the reign of Charles
II. If you have the right sort of hall, here is your hall
chair (see page 47): you can at least sit upon it.
Perhaps the same sort of purpose should be found for
the ART NOUVEAU chair, only in this case it will be
best if your house was built during, and representative
of, that brief flowering of originality in English
architecture between 1900 and 1910.

Other chairs in our little group are usual enough.

Left: Sewing; *Right:* Prince of Wales

The *Balloon-back* chair was popular throughout the Victorian age, and so was the padded armchair. Our specimen shows the *Prince of Wales* style, with its segments of padding representing feathers. The *Victoria* had a looped and waisted back with wooden padded arms; the *Prince Albert* was similar, only with a slightly bowed cresting; the *Princess Adelaide* had no arms, like the *Sewing* chair shown.

Finally our drawings show a chair which I have called 'Victoria Fireside'. It is in every junk shop; it is a cross between an armchair and a hall chair, though it was obviously meant for the fireside. It has rows of little bobbins and a carved cresting rail: and as it stands it looks horrible and you can have it for ten bob. Only I just wonder how it would look stripped and painted white, with simple pastel covering.

What other chairs are there? Well, we have said nothing about the *Bergère* chair, comfortably wide with external woodwork or rattan. We owe this origin-

ally to the France of LOUIS XV (although Chippendale
insisted on anglicizing the word to 'burjar'. An even
wider version of it was called a *Marquise* (see page 134).
The *Prie Dieu* chair, with its low seat and armrests
on the back, seems to be as useful for sitting as for
kneeling: and reproductions are sometimes found of
the *Farthingale* chair, with low back and no arms, for
my lady to perch her bolsterings upon. There are
chairs in WICKER WARE, and a *Beehive* chair made of
woven rush.

There are also all those others which one can only call
'fancy chairs', in all kinds of irrelevant styles, mainly
for bedrooms, nurseries and odd rooms, painted or
carved in every sort of style from LOUIS XV to Grecian,
from VICTORIAN Sheraton to William IV Edwardian. The
only combination I have not yet seen is a JAPANESQUE
adaptation of GOTHIC, but there is always hope.

All the same, you can count upon one thing. 'Contemporary' and 'genuine reproduction' have such a
hold on us now that unless these amusing and sometimes very charming little chairs become so sought
after as to call for reproduction, they will never be
made again nor be obtainable so cheaply. And they
are just right for your daughter's bedroom – before
she grows up and gets all 'contemporary'.

Charms

Anyone who expects his house to fall in or an earth-
quake to swallow him up might consider making a
collection of the various sorts of charms used to ward
off these and other evils. We still, if we are female,
wear them on our bangles and wristlets, though nowadays they seem to be mostly lovers' tokens, or little
vintage motor cars – there are, by the way, 'vintage'
versions of these, by which I mean charms in silver

which are contemporary with what we now call the 'vintage' car. But the watch-chainless man of today tends also to be going about without adequate protection: so perhaps we can find a few items in the junk shop.

Horse brasses, of course, had their origin as amulets or charms, the blinding 'sunflash' on the horse's forehead helping to ward off the 'evil eye' in days when, eerily enough, many people seem to have had this unpleasant attribute. One of these in the porch will keep away such folk, while a horseshoe over the door will help with an outbreak of fire, for if you leave it open end up it is symbolically holding water. Sometimes a dealer will offer you a piece of unicorn horn mounted in Chinese silver; but this is not likely to be unicorn – perhaps rhinoceros horn or the tusk of a narwhal, but either way it will assure you of everlasting happiness.

Pilgrims' tokens and religious MEDALS, of course, have their devotees, but you must make sure that you have not picked up some which having started life as deceptions will presumably have an adverse

Holed stone cattle charm and corn dolly
harvest charm

rather than a beneficial effect. 'Touchstones' are useful, not only for assessing the genuineness of precious metals, but for warding off scrofula, especially if worn on a white silk ribbon. If you happen to be a farmer, be sure to get one of those stones with holes in them sometimes found in the curio box; hung up in the cowshed or pigsty with your initials scratched on it it will make it no longer necessary to call in your vet to ailing animals.

A good representative collection of Chinese porcelain will be invaluable. Nothing represented in Chinese art ever really contains evil. The dragon, seen on pottery everywhere, symbolises the renewal of life, the tortoise longevity, the 'cash' or coin with a hole in it will bring riches, a leaping carp ensures that you pass your examinations.

For other possibilities in this department, it might be worth looking at the HUNDRED ANTIQUES, EIGHT IMMORTALS, RICE GRAIN PORCELAIN, BELLARMINES.

Chasing and Chased
A form of REPOUSSÉ work.

Chessmen
There are not only collectors of chess sets, but dealers who specialise in them. This is as well, for they have been made in so many parts of the world – even if our form of chess is not necessarily played there – that it takes some specialist expertise to assign them to a country of origin or a period – they did not follow general movements of styles.

There are, of course, the 'traditional' sets, but this is a word which seems to get tacked on to any style after it has been repeated for any length of time. Islam, for example, which forbids the representation

of the human figure, makes its own Sunnite chessmen'
which look like a lot of pepper pots or cabbage drain-
ers. The Chinese, who have a game of their own, play
it with discs placed on the corners of the squares: but
all the same they make 'traditional' ones for Europe,
and from Canton come most of those handsome sets
specially made for export, the pieces mounted on the
ivory BALL-IN-A-BALL, one side being white, the other
red. 'Portuguese' ones were also made by the Chinese,
but in Macao, the Portuguese treaty port, and here
the pawns are infantrymen of that nation in sixteenth-
century uniform. Sometimes the 'kings' were Napoleon, or the monarch of whatever country the set was
to be sold in.

European countries also had their 'traditional' types.
There was, for example, the 'St George' type, imported here from France; while our own 'Staunton'
sets, the ones most seen nowadays, are named after
the first Englishman to win the world championship.
Another English type was made by the Hastilow
family, their 'signature' being a fluting in the plinths
of the pieces.

Not all sets are in ivory: the priceless ones were
made in semi-precious stones, but there are others in
cast-iron, in wood, either plain or painted. The Black
Forest and the Tyrol have sent us carved and painted
ones of this sort, the pawns being tradesmen or
peasants.

French prisoners of war in this country made bone
chessmen; there are porcelain sets from Vienna and
Meissen; while our own English potteries, like Castleford and Wedgwood, also made them. The Wedgwood set was designed by Flaxman in jasper ware,
with the famous actress Mrs Siddons as the queen.
This latter is pretty rare, but I saw at a sale the other

day a set modelled after this, one side being in black basaltes, the other in white porcelain: in spite of extra kings, castles, bishops and knights, there were two pawns missing – so it made less than twenty pounds.

Enthusiasts tell me that unless you are simply collecting odd pieces for their interest, you should never, never buy incomplete sets in the hope of one day picking up the missing item: as with odd volumes, you almost never do.

Children's Furniture

Nobody can escape giving a little yelp of joy when they see one of those charming little pieces designed for the children of other days.

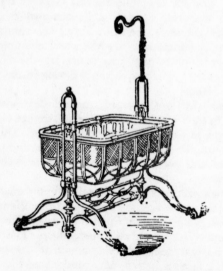

Edwardian swinging cot – 'the Pomona'

First there are the cradles, sometimes yielded up unwillingly by a farmhouse or cottage where it has done duty for generations. In this case, probably, it will be tougher and cruder in make, for they had to be shoved around on a stone floor used by the whole family and the neighbours as well. All the same, it might often be beautifully carved, perhaps with the initials of the fond parents, or their first offspring. These are on rockers, like the ones in wicker with a hood; but there are others which swing upon supports. From early Victorian days there is a model which has a clockwork rocking mechanism: it keeps going for forty-three minutes even now. And very occasionally one sees a specimen of those upholstered, silk and satin affairs, with canopies and draperies, which the late Victorians and Edwardians loved to use.

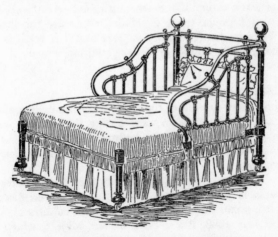

Edwardian child's half-size brass bedstead

Children's high chairs come in the styles of their period, either following country Windsor types, or town fashions; but there is also a variety which consists of a little chair mounted on the seat of an adult chair, or on a small table – which can be detached and put in front of the little chair when the occupant is not sitting up at the big table. Most of these look pretty practical, but when the artist designers came on the scene they sometimes let their ideas run away with them. There is an ART NOUVEAU high chair which is so top heavy that it probably explains why children reared at that time preferred to buy reproduction Sheraton when they grew up.

Another item of nursery furniture, of course, is the device for ensuring that the little one does not stray too far, or fall in the fire. Baby cages, on casters, helped the little mite to climb up on to its feet, and there is another sort which envelopes the child round the waist rather like a wooden crinoline on wheels.

But I prefer the high chairs, especially the little Windsor ones (*v. Looking in Junk Shops*). A chair is a chair, but a child's chair is something you want to put your child in.

Chip Carving

Junk shops are full of the work of the amateur craftsman, proudly kept in view during the maker's lifetime, then banished to a bedroom or an attic, then finally cleared out at a move or a death. *Ars longa vita brevis.*

One home activity, apparently a precursor of fretwork, is chip carving, which, in its post-medieval form, seems to have broken out in this country about the year 1888. But a book on the subject, which I have just borrowed from the public library, was taken

Whitewood tray traced for chip carving

out no fewer than six times in 1960, so it appears that the chip carver is still in the land.

Our wooden tray gives some idea of this work, which consists of so chipping the surface of a piece of wood that a shallow pattern results. It differs from carving proper in that the pattern is not in relief but in a series of V-notches. As in the case of POKER WORK, white wood goods like boxes, racks, WATCH HOLDERS, wall brackets, key racks, picture frames, etc., were traced for chip carving, and the worker used a knife or chisels to make the simple triangular cuts. But the more ambitious of them worked out their own designs, thus emulating the Scandinavian, Oriental and Maori work, examples of which one sometimes sees. Some very fine and free designs were produced by these methods.

Christmas Cards

Boxes and albums in junk sheds are there to be ransacked and made to yield their unconsidered treasures. Among these can be found letters, postcards, old photographs, VALENTINES – and Christmas cards. The *Art Journal* in 1889 said, 'The fashion of Christmas cards is on the wane.' How wrong can you be?

Victorian Christmas card

Why should anyone be interested in Christmas cards? I think the best answer to that is to look at a gathering of them – there are collections in various museums – representative of different periods in the 120 years of their existence. The first fact that comes up and hits you is that here, if anywhere, is an entirely popular art. This was what the public, all sections of it, really liked, otherwise they wouldn't have bought them.

What they bought all through these years has an astounding range. There are, of course, robins, snow, holly, Father Christmases, stage coaches and the rest; but there are also charming little vignettes of early Victorian children, beautiful flower paintings and landscapes, some rather surprising nudes and semi-nudes of adolescents, and fearful warnings about taking the Lord's name in vain; Kate Greenaway's popular little misses and masters in their 'never-never' land costumes; topical cards showing such excitements as the early motor cars; cards from the fighting fronts of various wars, comic humanised animals; cards like cheques so that you could request the Bank of Blessings to pay to the order of the recipient

'Two Thousand Joys'; trick cards with a tab which
sets angels bobbing up and down; fold-out tableaux
of the Nativity. They come in silk and satin, are
trimmed with lace and even dried grasses and seaweed; some even have little dabs of cotton wool which
once bore a drop of some long-vanished perfume.

The history of the Christmas card was first told
in a special number of the *Studio* for 1894 by Gleeson
White, whose work on the Victorian illustrators is
well-known. But on this occasion White was rather
solemn, objecting to 'unlovely objects', and 'practical
jokes of the lowest order'; he didn't even like the
robins very much. Not so Mr Buday (see READING
LIST), who takes in and hugely enjoys everything
the Christmas card has to offer. If you decide to
collect them, let him be your guide; if not, read his
book for its absorbing little sidelights on the tastes and
interests over the last century.

Can we trace the first commercially published
Christmas card? Oddly enough, it seems we can.
It was designed by J. C. Horsley, an R.A.-to-be, and
published in 1843. About 1,000 copies were sold at a
shilling each, and it showed a convivial Dickensian
family scene such as occurred on a memorable Christmas at Dingley Dell. This was severely criticised, says
Mr Buday, as being likely to encourage drunkenness.

Since then, as noted, the diversity of cards has been
immense. You can find among them the words of such
writers as W. S. Gilbert, Christina Rosetti, Robert
Louis Stevenson, George Eliot, Lord Tennyson, Lewis
Carroll, and many shy souls who hide their identity
under initials – how interesting to ferret them out and
find some 'important' writers among them! As artists
you can have Phil May, Kate Greenaway, Sargent,
among thousands of others.

E

And it still goes on: in recent years you have had the choice cards by Sir Alfred Munnings, Winston Churchill – and Picasso. What more could an art collector want?

Coconut Cups

No great rarities are the more modest versions of the old coconut cup. Our ancestors were always fascinated by exotic fruits like the pineapple and the coconut, and when the latter arrived here it must have struck them as a very handy substitute for the 'mazer' or wooden ceremonial cup.

So after cutting it in half and polishing it to a shining dark brown they mounted it with a silver rim and stand, and perhaps a shield or some other decoration. With very grand ones, the smaller half would be turned into a lid, also with its silver mount.

My own humble specimen, a chubby friendly little lidless cup bearing the date 1808 and the initials of a donor and a recipient, came as a gift, but with such a modest amount of silver it would not have cost a great deal: this was doubtless one reason for their popularity all the way from the fifteenth to the nineteenth century – and probably also the reason why so many have survived the melting pot. One sometimes also finds coconuts as a goblet mounted with ivory; and they are also known in the form of POWDER FLASKS.

Late-18th-century silver-mounted coconut cup

I have heard that once upon a time a coconut cup was thought to have magical powers, that wine drunk out of it would cure aches and pains.

Commode

What is a commode? The first thing it is not is a night commode: this was a Victorian revival, for a special purpose, of a term which a century before they might have applied to a chest-of-drawers.

So what is the difference between a commode and a chest-of-drawers? It is a good question, for there are commodes with drawers which *look* just like rather splendid chests-of-drawers.

This, I think, gives the clue: at any rate it is my rough criterion. A commode is first of all one of those magnificent pieces of furniture which started life in France as a free-standing chest with drawers or doors,

Louis xv commode

or both. We borrowed the word (anything French being highly fashionable) to describe the more stately forms of the chest-of-drawers we had been evolving quietly since the Restoration.

The place for the commode, with its priceless lacquering or marquetry or whatnot, was in the drawing-room: the more restrained, but still very elegant, chest-of-drawers was for the bedroom.

Corkscrews

To be caught with a fine bottle of burgundy and without a corkscrew is a sad business, and is probably the reason men turn into corkscrew collectors. Corkscrews have been with us since the days of the first Queen Elizabeth, and were originally called bottle-screws, like the devices in ship's riggings named after them. Once upon a time, it appears, after staying with someone who had a particularly good cellar, it was considered polite to send him a handsome corkscrew in silver engraved with his crest or a word of praise.

Corkscrews come in enormous variety, and look astonishingly well when they are mounted on a framed board. There are carved ones in wood and bone, delicate little silver ones for the eighteenth-century

'Wier's Patent' nickel-plated corkscrew

gentleman's pocket, perhaps combined with an ear-pick and a firesteel. 'King's' screws have a socket which fits over the neck of the bottle and of course there is the reverse screw for delicate handling of the crusted port. Ladies needed corkscrews for their miniature scent bottles, cellarmen for their stone jars.

In the last century invention ran riot, and it would be an absorbing task in more ways than one to seek out all these clever ideas and try them on your bottles.

Cornucopia

Or 'Horn of Plenty' (*cornu*: horn; *copiæ*: full). This famous symbol, showing a goat's horn overflowing with fruit, flowers and corn, comes to us from classical times, these bountiful things being showered upon mortals by such friendly personages as Plutus, Fortuna and others.

Potters and metalworkers all down the variegated

Caughley blue and white porcelain cornucopia

years have seized upon it to make a shapely receptacle for the wall or the table and to describe all its forms would be merely to catalogue these wares.

It is mentioned here as a decorative and pretty well inexhaustible possibility for the collector who likes to collect by theme or shape.

Cries of London

If you have never seen this famous set of prints in anything but a modern reproduction you may be astonished to find how much better the originals are. They were published between 1793 and 1797 by the still existing firm of Colnaghi, and come from thirteen paintings by Francis Wheatley, a Dublin portrait painter who came to London when Irish society turned up their noses at him for living with a lady who was not his wife.

The prints were never actually engraved by BARTOLOZZI, but the 'Cries' stand with his work among the most popular examples of the eighteenth-century stipple print; and however mauled they may be in inferior reproduction they have far more real atmosphere than most of this *genre*. Some discerning collectors prefer to find them not coloured, but in 'bistre', a brown pigment which captures more faithfully the subtleties of light and shade in the original pictures.

Those who would like to see more of Wheatley's work should look out for his 'Soldier's Return', 'Sailor's Return', 'The Disaster', and wholly charming pieces like 'The Cottage Door', 'The School Door' and 'Setting out for the Fair'. As with any other eighteenth-century prints, they can be bought in fine 'early states', in later impressions, and in reproductions, depending on what you want to spend.

Cuckoo Clocks

If you want a piece of Victorian 'Gothic' in its most romantic mood (see VICTORIAN STYLES) you can hardly do better than try to get one of the early cuckoo clocks, with their touching landscapes surrounded by carving.

The cuckoo clock is said to have been invented by

Franz Anton Ketterer (1676–1750), a native of the Black Forest in Germany; and from there it spread all over the world. The very earliest ones are quite simple and unadorned, after which they picked up the romantically painted scenes. It was much later that they turned themselves into the hunting lodges or chalets, with overhanging gables, that we know today. Some, apart from the cuckoo, have a musical box, and there may be a quail calling the quarters.

Cup Bordes and Side Boardes

Here we must tread very carefully, for such high controversy still rages about such terms as court cupboards, livery cupboards, aumbries and the like, even among the experts, that mere tasters like you and me can easily get into a tangle.

Much of the confusion seems to have arisen because these various things could be used for different purposes at different times, with the result that you have contemporary accounts which flatly contradict each other. All the same, every piece of furniture starts by having a purpose, so let us try to see what were the purposes of these things.

To begin with, it will be noted that the names given above are all of French origin – though it is the French of Plantagenet England rather than the French of France. That being so, it has been argued that the *Court Cupboard* must have been a *short* cupboard: but court cupboards can be huge affairs. They could, of course, have been used mainly at Court, though the evidence is all against it. Personally, I wonder if they do not have something to do with the manorial courts held in the lord's hall, or the local Guildhall. I have been in several old manor houses, small castles and town halls, where there is a 'courtroom'; so why not 'court cupboards', for the display of special regalia?

But whatever their original purpose we know that this sort of open cupboard ('cup bordes' were always simply open shelves in the beginning) was used for the display of pewter and delftware plates and dishes, flagons and the like – and there was often a carpet or piece of tapestry draped over the top shelf; the drinking pots were kept on the lowest shelf – the 'pot borde'. These were in use right down to the reign of Charles II and even probably later.

Some Court cupboards have lockers on the middle shelf, sometimes only one, sometimes three, the outside ones being recessed. These lockers were called *Aumbries* – in fact the medieval name for a closed cupboard – the English name was a *Hutch* (though still from the French *Huche!*). In this one would, presumably, lock away the costly ornate silver, though in some accounts this also seems to have been displayed outside.

Then we have the so-called *Livery Cupboard*. Mr Gordon Roe has very sensibly suggested that this word might well be dropped altogether. First of all it has nothing at all to do with 'livery' in the sense of a uniform, which many people assume it has. The word

Left: Court, living or buffet; *Right:* Linen or clothes press

Left: Welsh tridarn; *Right:* Open Court

comes from the French *livrée*, which some authorities
(wrongly, I think) translate as 'delivered'; but which
seems to my mind to tie up most convincingly with
the original meaning of 'livery' which was, according
to the OED, 'to dispense food, provisions, and clothing
to retainers or servants'. We know from contemporary
accounts that a livery cupboard was used for the
'livery', or what we would call the rations, of bread,
wine and ale provided for the staff of a large house.
But I think these references are to what had formerly
been called a Court cupboard, and had now acquired
lockers because of the replacing of pewter by such
costly items as glasses. The *Buffet* seems to have been
exactly the same article of furniture, but called by
the modern French name which had become 'U' in
the eighteenth century: the OED's first reference is
dated 1720. All the same, I have a suspicion that the
real livery cupboards and buffets were those with
pierced decoration in the panels and the lockers: how
else would one keep the food fresh?

What does seem to be an entirely different article of
furniture – and therefore a name worth more usage
than auctioneers and dealers commonly give it – is
the *Press*. Here both the upper and lower shelves are

completely enclosed by doors, the upper doors usually being recessed to form a narrow shelf. The place for this was not the dining hall, but the bedroom, where it held clothes and linen. In Wales these sometimes occur with quite high upper cupboards, and have picked up the name, apparently from Victorian days, of 'Top-hat Cupboards'.

The reader may well wonder why one has spent so much time with such medieval-sounding items of furniture, but in fact there are a good many of them about, even in junk shops. One reason is that along with DRESSERS such articles continued to be made for the farmhouse and the smaller manor house long after people in the higher echelons of society had gone in for *Cabinets*, *Tallboys* and other elegances: and they are still sometimes to be found in their original villages. The other reason is that among the VICTORIAN STYLES one finds re-creations of these early forms: they gave wonderful opportunities for the heavy and intricate carving so beloved of the era, and the workmanship is so good that it takes a sharp eye to know in just which century of about four they might have been made.

Left: Bacon cupboard and settle; *Right:* Queen Anne tallboy

Close relations to the *Press*, one supposes, are the Welsh two-piece and three-piece cupboards known as the *Cwpwrdd Deuddarn* and *Cwpwrdd Tridarn* respectively. In some of the former the topmost section was open; in the latter there could be drawers as well as small lockers.

What other sorts of cupboards are there? Well, we all know the *Corner* cupboard in its various forms, with either panelled or glazed doors, and many a nice collection of china they hold. Another sort is the pleasant little *Spice* cupboard with its drawers for herbs, simples and other items which not only flavoured the food but cured the colic and other ills.

There is also the *Bacon* cupboard, which is a sort of SETTLE (see page 69), being a seat backed by a cupboard having hooks on which you hung your bacon after curing. Today these sit very well in a hall, to hide all those shabby mackintoshes and hats.

*

Sideboards, as we have seen, could well have started with the Court cupboard or the 'livery' table: they could also by acquiring shelves become DRESSERS. But there was also a type of sideboard which is much more clearly the ancestor of the present type, that is the *Credence*, used for the holy vessels in churches. They simply looked like the bottom half of a dresser with cupboard doors and drawers over. Later on the cupboards were dropped, but the drawers retained and you had the typical JACOBEAN sideboard with barley-sugar legs and several small drawers for the cutlery.

In Chippendale's time there was the pleasant SER-PENTINE-fronted 'side table' which straightened itself out under Hepplewhite and Sheraton. In late Georgian days this would be flanked with urns and pedestals in the manner of ADAM (see pp 7–9) and there could be two tiers of drawers though still with plenty of daylight below them. In REGENCY days the cupboards returned and went right down to the floor again, as they had in the Credence, and thus there evolved our massive Victorian sideboards, sometimes with a Break-front (see page 221), or the Chiffonier.

In the present century the sideboard has gone up on legs again and we are back to something like the eighteenth century. This is consequently as good a place as any to record one's pleasure in the work of designers of the immediate yesterday, like Ernest Gimson, Gordon Russell and Sydney Barnsley, also the early Heal designs: they were particularly good in the way they rescued the sideboard from some of its Victorian excesses.

Damascening

This is something to look for on fine metalwork. It consists of gold or silver wire inlaid into a baser metal like steel, iron or bronze: the design is CHASED first and the wire hammered into the grooves.

The name arises because of an association with the swordsmiths of Damascus. In its early days it was used a great deal on swords, shields and armour, for although fighting men always wanted their arms to be in the toughest sort of metal they also liked a brave display: damascening gave them this.

In later days, of course, it comes in all sorts of forms: boxes, vases, salvers, knives, scissors, and especially much Indian work like the old koftgari shields. BIDRI WARE is a sort of damascening, and there is another kind which has the pattern etched with acid and the work laid in with gold leaf.

Dish Covers

There was a time when the large Sheffield Plate or ELECTRO-PLATE – even to some extent the Silver – dish cover was loafing about in the shops waiting vainly for a buyer: it seemed so clumsy that there was nothing on earth to be done with it. Well, the silver ones were always worth their value as silver, now pretty high, but what of the others: has a use been found for them?

Yes, it has. Turn it upside-down and hang it on wires and you have a handsome hanging basket for flowers or plants. Cut it in half and you have *two* handsome wall brackets, also for flowers. Vandalism? Yes, but what else can you do with them; they can be bought for thirty shillings.

One interesting point to look for if you get a Sheffield Plate one is the shield. Many owners like to have the arms or initials inscribed on their tableware, and as Sheffield Plate is only a layer of silver fused on to a copper base, any engraving would have gone through to the copper. So they inserted on one side of the cover near the rim a little shield in solid silver which would take the engraving. You can spot this usually by its brightness.

These covers can also be found, by the way, in BRITANNIA METAL, with an ELECTRO-PLATED handle.

Doctor Syntax

This character is to be found on a famous set of Staffordshire plates by R. and J. Clews, of Cobridge, and though they have long been collected, odd ones turn up and puzzle those who may not be acquainted with the learned Doctor and his extraordinary adventures.

Even more extraordinary, though, is the way these adventures came to be written. The scenes on the

19th-century 'Dr Syntax' tureen

plates come from drawings made by Thomas Rowlandson. He, or a friend of his, had the idea of doing a book which would make fun of the popular 'picturesque travels' books of the day: and Ackermann the publisher, though he put out such books himself, liked the notion. Looking for an author, he found a hack writer named William Coomb who had for many years been shut up in the King's Bench prison for debt – he was there for forty-three years altogether – and commissioned him to write the verses to fit the pictures. Neither Rowlandson nor Coomb were very reliable workers, so as each monthly part was wanted for a magazine, the publisher had to send someone to Rowlandson and stand over him while he did a picture; and then go on to Coomb in his prison cell and stand beside him until he had written the necessary verse. Coomb never knew what sort of picture would be coming next and had to make up his story as he went along. In fact, it was not for some years, until the series was well established, that author and illustrator ever met.

The pictures on the plates – there are about eighty in all and they have been done by other potters as well – are from three of the books: *Dr Syntax in Search of the Picturesque*, which came out in 1815; *The Second Tour of Dr Syntax*, published in 1820; and *Dr Syntax in Search of a Wife*, published in the following year.

They relate the comic adventures of a curate school-master who, though quite a dignified and likeable character, gets into endless scrapes. On the back of his old mare Grizzle he gets mixed up with a cavalry review; is chased by bulls, robbed, pitched into duck-ponds, mistakes a private house for an inn, and so on. The verses, written in an ambling style, are still quite readable, so if you are going to collect these plates it is worth getting the books.

Dogs of Fo

I do not know if the owners of Pekinese dogs will feel outraged if I compare their darlings with the animal shown on this page, but I am assured that there is a connection.

For these are Dogs of Fo, sometimes called Lions of Fo, sometimes the Lion Dogs of China. Their job was to stand guard on either side of the gates of Buddhist temples. Personally, if I were a Pekinese, I would feel very deeply complimented by being compared with one of these ferocious little animals.

These figures, usually in green enamel porcelain with decoration in other colours, including aubergine, are often to be seen, and are nice to have. They have been made since Ming (1368–1644) times, but the

Dog of Fo

earlier ones will cost you a packet. The female plays with a puppy of the species: the male plays with a ball – but keeps his eye on you.

Don't confuse these – as auctioneers sometimes do – with kylins. These are fabulous animals with a deer's body, scales all over it, and a large bushy head: they are said to embody the Perfect Good. Not surprisingly, therefore, they are rarely found.

Dressers

Everyone likes a fine dresser, set out with its china or glass, or sometimes gleaming pewter. There are still a good many about if you take the trouble to look for them, and considering the workmanship to be found in them I would not call them dear. I have seen excellent early-nineteenth-century oak and mahogany ones go for forty or fifty pounds, which does not seem a lot for the principal piece of furniture and base for decoration in the living-room of a cottage or a small country house.

Before looking at the different sorts of dressers, let us consider its origin. The word comes from the Norman French *dresseur*, which meant that the original dresser was really a sideboard (see CUP BORDES AND SIDE BOARDES) on which one 'dressed' the food before serving it. Later you had that division of purpose whereby the large houses elaborated their sideboards, and perhaps displayed their fine pieces on a Court cupboard; whereas the smaller establishment, such as a farmhouse with a general-purpose living-room, would be more likely to let the dresser acquire shelves for their scoured pewter, blue and white delftware, and perhaps the brown Staffordshire slipware. In some parts of the country, in fact, a dresser is sometimes called a delft-rack, the shelves being built in the walls.

Dresser with serpentine shelves (*top*), 'Country Georgian' dresser (*left*) and north country dresser (*right*)

Now for the types. Much has been written about regional types of dressers, but when one gets down to it and looks at those which are still in the houses where they started life perhaps two hundred years ago, one has to be pretty wary about laying down rules. The 'Welsh' dresser is well-known, and there is certainly a distinctive type, but I think this word 'Welsh' is often used of any dresser simply because there are probably more surviving in Wales than anywhere else. But the Welsh and West Country (including Cornish) dresser seems generally to be a compact affair with a backboard, often with pierced apron work, or an arched gallery over the upper shelf. They are sometimes covered with red lead and painted black to protect them from damp and pests. Often there are narrow cupboards at the sides of the shelves in others there may be a clock in the centre flanked by spice drawers.

Quite a different sort of dresser is found on the other side of the country. With an open back there are rails along the dresser front to keep the plates in and often the shelves are free-standing. These seem to be common in Yorkshire and Lancashire. There is yet another, which I suspect of having East Anglian affinities – because of a certain 'Dutch' feeling; there is a high arched top and the shelves have bobbin railings.

Still another variety does not seem to have local tendencies at all, but has moved out of the kitchen into the sitting-room and acquired cabriole legs, SERPENTINE front, and the graceful though simple lines of what is known as 'Country Georgian'. These dressers could hold their own with any sort of furniture, and they are naturally much more expensive than the others.

But – to revert to the 'kitchen' type dresser – if I wanted one badly and could not find one at the right price I would be very much inclined to go back to origins by looking for a good oak side-table with drawers and/or cupboards, and then build my shelving over it. Using old wood, you would have something not at all different from the 'dressers' to be found in many a country kitchen today.

Dummy Board Figures

Just occasionally you will see in one of the better-class shops a cut-out figure, sometimes life-size, sometimes only three or four feet high, of a person in seventeenth- or more likely eighteenth- and early-nineteenth-century costume. There are shepherds and shepherdesses, housemaids with brooms, soldiers, ladies brushing their hair, boys and girls playing, and domestic animals like dogs and cats.

Once upon a time these figures were to be found in private houses all over the country, in tea gardens,

17th-century **dummy board figure**

coffee houses and inns. Why, nobody seems very sure. They certainly stood in front of empty fireplaces in summertime: being of wood, they could not have been used when the fire was alight. They also stood at the ends of corridors in large houses, and in the tea gardens they were generally disposed so that you came on them by surprise, as with a ha-ha. There is also a theory that they were left in windows to hoodwink possible housebreakers. Probably they were there just for fun, or for companionship.

Eggs

Children get chocolate eggs for Easter now, but once upon a time you gave them real ones which were charmingly painted with a picture and sometimes a name. Boiled very hard, they were put away in a cupboard to be kept as mementoes. Later the potters made them in china and earthenware, and some of these have floral sprays, some pictures of birds, animals and ships. I found one only the other day which divided in half; it was in Copenhagen porcelain and it cost me three shillings. Another class bears views of the town in which you bought them as a souvenir of a trip, and were made in Staffordshire, Sunderland and other places.

19th-century china presentation egg

Another race of eggs in china and glass, painted with more conventional designs, were used as hand coolers, probably very necessary when you wore lots of clothes in stuffy rooms; and they were made also to use in darning. To put the thing completely in reverse, there were also hand *warmers*. These were hollow, with a silver screw top, filled with hot water, and were carried in the muff. A first cousin to this is the egg scent bottle, painted in the colours of actual birds' eggs, and therefore a wonderful subject for collecting.

Eight Immortals

This venerable band appear so often in ivory, porcelain, pictures, etc., that it may interest collectors to know something about them. They are (or were) to the Chinese what the saints are to European Catholics, and between them they represent the eight human states of youth, age, wealth, poverty, aristocracy, plebeianism, masculinity and femininity. They stand for the Taoist principles of contempt for material comforts and worldly power, and for the eternal longings of man for a world of faery. All the same, they are a very nice lot of people, with plenty of human traits – sometimes they are shown sitting in a glade having what we would call a glorious binge – and they thoroughly deserve their immortality. They lived at different periods over about a thousand years.

Generally accepted as the leading character is the fat man of the party, *Chung-Li Ch'uan*, sometimes represented as a general, but always with a fan. He used this to very good purpose, according to one account, when meeting a young widow who was busily fanning the freshly dug soil on her husband's grave: she had

Eight Immortals (*left to right*)
Chung-Li Ch'uan; Chang Kuo-hao; Li T'ieh-kuai;
Han Hsiang-tzu

a successor lined up, but could not marry him until her first husband's grave was dry. The general at once dried the grave for her by waving his magic fan.

More often seen perhaps is *Lu Tung-pin*, who wears a pleated cap, carries a sword on his back and also a fly whisk. His special interest is sick people, and shrines have been built to him. *Chang Kuo-hao* may be recognised as a bearded man carrying what looks astonishingly like a golfer's bag with two clubs in it: it is a drum made from a bamboo stick. This reverend gentleman had a very handy form of transport in the form of a white mule (he is sometimes shown sitting on it) which, after being ridden for a thousand miles or so, could be folded up and put in a wallet; he brought the mule into service again merely by pouring water over the wallet.

Ts'ao Kuo-chiu, a bearded man with the cap of a member of the Imperial Court, carries tickets of admission to the Court, but not caring much for parties he gave up the courtly life and became a mountain hermit. *Li T'ieh-kuai* is the beggar of the party, hideous and deformed, with an iron crutch and a

Lu Tung-pin; Ts'ao Kuo-chiu;
Ho Hsien-ku; Lan Ts'ai-ho

calabash or GOURD. He acquired his present appearance because at one time he was frequently being recalled to heaven for consultation, leaving his body on earth. After returning from one of these missions he found that someone, thinking him dead, had cremated him without making proper enquiries. However, the Immortal found the body of a lame beggar and used that. Not a difficult man to please.

Han Hsiang-tzu, like Orpheus, could spellbind even animals with his music, though he uses a flute rather

Shou Lao, star of longevity

than a lute, and is sometimes shown playing it. But he is also seen carrying the broken branch of a peach tree in memory of the occasion when he tried, but failed, to climb to immortality up the tree. He is the patron saint of musicians. *Lan Ts'ai-ho* is sometimes shown as a girl, sometimes as a youth, but either way the figure carries a basket or bouquet of flowers, and is associated with the idea of longevity. But the only veritable lady of the party is *Ho Hsien-ku*, a sort of celestial Cinderella, who had a bullying stepmother and is consequently shown either with a ladle filled with magic fungus, a lotus bloom, or a basket of wild flowers which she has had to gather in the mountains.

Sometimes you will see all eight Immortals going to an audience with the Star of Longevity, the venerable *Shou Lao*, who, with an enormous domed bald head, is himself a frequent figure in the shops.

Electro-plate

But surely not common or garden electro-plate! Could one possibly get interested in *that*?

I assure you, Sir and Madam, that just as people have long collected Sheffield Plate – substitute for solid sterling silver – so a few forward-looking persons are already seeking out early examples of the wares which put Sheffield Plate out of business. After all, the thing happened over a century ago, and that makes electro-plate in the eyes of the United States Customs at least as much an antique as a Renaissance bronze.

It was around the year 1840 that the still-famous firm of Elkingtons took out the basic patent for the process whereby a thin coating of silver or gold could be deposited upon a baser metal by electrolysis. It follows, therefore, that since most things in silver also came in electro-plate, pieces made throughout the Victorian era show all those entrancingly interesting mix-ups of motifs which are mentioned briefly under VICTORIAN STYLES.

Sometimes the base was of copper (as in Sheffield Plate – but see *Looking in Junk Shops*), sometimes of BRITANNIA METAL, but mostly of what was at first GERMAN SILVER, an alloy of copper, zinc and nickel, later modified into 'nickel silver', thus giving us the initials 'E.P.N.S.' – electro-plated nickel silver, which is usually stamped on the base of a piece.

Electro-plated teapot

It matters not if your early find is tarnished, or has lost most of its silver deposit; it can be stripped and re-silvered through your silversmiths. As noted under BRITANNIA METAL, the trade is already performing this service for you and offering the result in silver which is, as the advertisement says, whiter than white. They are also doing this to worn Sheffield Plate and to copper articles which started life as naked copper.

Embossing and Embossed
Another form of REPOUSSÉ work.

En Suite
Things are *en suite* with each other when they match, or go together, or form part of a set. Your chesterfield is usually en suite with two large armchairs, a GARNITURE DE CHEMINÉE gives you perhaps a clock, vases and other items *en suite* with each other. You can also have ear-rings, necklace and brooch made *en suite*.

Etagère
Some say this is another name for a WHATNOT, or tier of open shelves, supported by posts: others that it earns this name only when it lives on top of a sideboard or chiffonier. The nice ones are in ormolu, probably with galleries round the stages so that the precious little knick-knacks on it won't fall over the edge.

Façon de Venise
This is collector's language for a style of glassmaking which derives from Venice, either by fashion, or by emigrating glassmakers.

Unless we become collectors we are unlikely to have much to do with its manifestations in sixteenth- and seventeenth-century Netherlandish, German, and English glass, but we shall come across it in a form which one might more appropriately name 'Anglo-Venetian', or perhaps 'Stourbridge Venetian'.

This appears as ewers and jugs, decanters and glasses blown in a wavy form, often with striped colours and extra decoration in the shape of little raspberry 'prunts' or lozenges. It was our late nineteenth-century reaction from the rather stereotyped form of crystal – and the public loved it. To us, now, it looks pretty and engaging, and is well worth the pound or two asked for it.

'Façon de Venise' vase

Another, and posher, type makes use of the Venetian LATTICINIO decoration, with opaque white or coloured glass threading, which one sees in a more homely fashion in Nailsea glass (*v. Looking in Junk Shops*). But there are tall compotiers candles, and goblets which are Venetian in shape as well.

I note that such forms are being made available in the smart shops again today, presumably from Italy.

Famille Rose, Verte, Noire and Jaune

You will not look in shop windows for very long without coming across these styles of decoration in porcelain. Even if you do not see the original work from China, you are bound to find English adaptations of them on china, earthenware, etc., right down to Mason's Ironstone, which is still being produced.

Famille Rose is one of the great 'families' of Chinese porcelain enamelled in various colours – usually three or five. It gets its name from a certain rose pink which appears as one of the colours: and the other 'families' have similar dominant colours – Famille Verte (green), Famille Jaune (yellow), Famille Noire (black). The French names are due to their having first been appreciated and classified by collectors of that nationality.

It is also worth noting, perhaps, that the colour of Famille Rose is something which the Chinese, for a change, owe to Europe: it is produced from a gold

K'ang Hsi Famille Noire vase and Famille Verte vase

chloride called 'Purple of Cassius', after a Dutch chemist.

Many famous patterns derive from Famille Rose originals, notably the INDIAN TREE of Coalport, and patterns made today. If you go to museums and get these fixed in your mind, you will have some happy hours spotting them in all sorts of disguises.

Famille Verte is older than Famille Rose, carries much red and POWDER BLUE, and appears a lot in figures like the DOGS OF FO. The Famille Jaune and Famille Noire appear often as the ground colour of large jars, baluster vases, and 'rouleaux' or four-sided vases. The black ones, with flowers in yellow, green and white, are specially fine, but it should be noted that the original ones are not simply black: a transparent green wash has been floated over the black giving it a unique appearance.

In case you can't find original specimens of these 'families' at your prices, be it noted that the Crown Staffordshire Porcelain Company in the late nineteenth century made excellent reproductions of vases

Famille Rose plate

in the colours and styles of the Famille Verte and the Famille Rose, and also, incidentally, wares with POWDER BLUE grounds. There was no intention to deceive: the crown and 'Staffs' or 'Staffordshire' appears on every piece – if someone has not removed it.

Finger Plates

Obliging manufacturers are making for us replicas of finger plates which prevent us from making dirty marks where we push open doors; also indeed of the knobs and the furniture of the lock. It has always been possible, at a price, to pick up some genuine plates or knobs in porcelain or coloured glass; but why not take advantage of the much wider choice that these replicas will give you?

One might also mention in this place that in those mysterious shops which serve 'the trade' – and which can be reached through it – you can buy practically any kind of brass or ormolu fitting for drawers of whatever period you like, and restore your piece to its original style whenever you wish to.

Fire Insurance Signs

You will sometimes see on the walls of old houses, usually at about first-floor level, metal plaques bearing symbols, numbers and names. The 'Sun' is a frequent one; the 'Phoenix' another. They are fire insurance

Fire insurance sign

marks, and although collectors do not actually tear the houses down to get at them, they, or the local dealers, generally contrive to be around on demolition day.

These plaques date from the days when fire brigades were run by private enterprise (the insurance offices), which meant that when a fire broke out the firemen elected to save the properties they had insured, and cheerfully left the rest to burn to the ground. Presumably they had a team of salesmen on the spot offering plaques to the improvident.

Originally the plaques bore the actual policy number, and these are the ones which are eagerly snapped up. Tin, iron, copper and zinc were used for most of them, but some are in TERRA COTTA, and porcelain, or were even on a stone built into the house.

In 1833, when these various guerilla brigades started to combine into a public service, the strict necessity for the plaques ended, and even the uninsured could get their fires put out. But the plaques continued in use as advertisements until about 1860.

Fitted Boxes and Cases
By this I mean not the hundreds of little patch and snuff boxes, BONBONNIÈRES and so on, but real containers fitted with contents for some special purpose.

Let me give you two examples. There is the apothecary's box, with lots of fascinating little compartments and drawers containing bottles, phials, pestle and mortar, and various other tricks of the trade. Also I recently saw a barber's box with three swivel compartments having ivory fittings, scissors, pewter soapbox, etc.

Hat-boxes often turn up, sometimes with a top hat either lay or ecclesiastical; and there are many ribbon

Apothecary's cabinet

boxes with their mechanical winders. Thread boxes and workboxes, of course, are among the many interesting items associated with needlework.

There are other sorts of boxes which I suppose one should really call cases, such as those used for comfort on long coach journeys. They are elegant affairs in morocco leather, either with a complete tea service or spirit bottles and glasses, with writing materials, or toilet requisites: there are also complete 'coach' baskets containing almost everything of this sort.

Only produce one of these at a picnic, at the races, or on some other outing and you will have all your friends drooling over the fine workmanship and quality which went into its making.

Flambé
Like SANG DE BOEUF, this is another of the copper glazes created in Chinese porcelain in the K'ang Hsi era, and, like it too, was successfully revived in late nineteenth-century English pottery. Its red is streaked or veined with grey, purple, lavender, blue, etc.

Flower Pots and Pedestals
It is always rather a mystery to me that when, after being overlooked for many years, something is wanted

it suddenly appears as if by magic. Where has it been hidden all this time? The mystery thickens when it comes to those large Victorian plant pots and holders, some of them standing on pedestals, which are now to be seen in serried ranks outside the country junk shops. These must have been very difficult indeed to hide, so one can only suppose that there are a lot more conservatories and unmodernised houses about than one had imagined.

Wrought-iron flower stand for window or fireplace

Anyway there they are, and people with a fresh eye for Victoriana are buying them to put in their small town backyards or on terraces in their gardens. And when you come to look at them they are really something in the way of potting. This was 'art pottery' in its day, and firms really went to town with pots in their rich 'majolica' glazes, in stoneware with incised decoration or moulded in leaf shapes; also in ware in which fabric patterns were impressed upon the wet clay. Copeland produced pedestals in blue and white which are quite five feet high; others are more modest affairs, urn or vase shaped. BURMAN-TOFTS, makers of tiles, were also in this field, and their name is often found on the bottoms of jardinières.

Coming to the table, one often sees all the little

white table decorations in china moulded as leaves, or with bowls supported by cherubs or prettily dressed children, rather like those in Mary Gregory Glass (*v. Looking in Junk Shops*). There were also window flower stands in pleasantly convoluted wrought-iron whereby you could suspend your earthenware pots three at a time, either in line or echelon.

These are to be found, all nicely painted for you at rather staggering prices, but my advice to you is to ask friends with old greenhouses or outbuildings to let you poke around and see what you can find. There are also sometimes some interesting things of this sort at the back of old blacksmiths' shops.

Food Warmers and Heaters

What a great many different things have been used at different times to keep our food warm by day or night, at the table or by the bedside. I wonder how many of them are still known to a generation, the greater part of which, when at home, eats its food only a yard or two from the place where it was cooked.

Aristocrat of the species I suppose is the *Veilleuse*, or *Réchaud* (in France), *Suppenwärmer* (in Germany), *Scaldavivande* (in Italy), and *Food Warmer* (in England). It is a simple enough contrivance, consisting

Wedgwood creamware tea warmer

Electro-plated **egg steamer**, with revolving top and 'rustic' mounts

of a bowl and cover suspended in a stand which has an opening for a *godet* or lamp. It therefore provided not only heat for the POSSET, CAUDLE, or whatever was left by the bedside, but light as well. How did the smoke and fumes get out? There are vents under the handles on either side. The earliest of them were in eighteenth-century delftware and porcelain, all elaborately decorated in the styles of the day, but plainer versions appear in the creamware (*v. Looking in Junk Shops*) not only of our own Josiah Wedgwood but of his imitators on the Continent. If you try to collect a *veilleuse* in the Marché aux Puces at the weekend, bear in mind the warning of Mr Harold Newman, the authority on these things, that they are quite likely to be brand new.

Next we have the *Tea Warmer* in which Wedgwood was also implicated, whereby a kettle takes the place of the soup bowl: there is a handsome gilt and painted specimen in porcelain from Paris (Clignancourt) in the Victoria and Albert Museum, which also has a red earthenware Staffordshire and a creamware Leeds kettle which have apparently lost their pedestals.

The *Warming Plate* calls for mention. These are to be found in many places, in Staffordshire blue and white: I bought one with a Spode 'Caramanian' pattern on it not so long ago for eight shillings. It is a plate of double thickness, having a small aperture just under the rim into which you pour hot water, or, I believe, hot sand. There are Chinese versions of this about too, some of them having holes to attach a cover. I am told that there are others with two foot-rings close to each other so that the plate can fit over a bowl of hot water or sand.

From the tea kettle to the *Tea-maker*, shaped like an egg which you drop into the pot: how long ago is it that we gave up making tea in this terribly un-English way? They were certainly being sold by Harrods in 1900 – perhaps foreigners bought them. Then there are egg steamers, silver or ELECTRO-PLATED, with revolving tops and rustic mounts elegantly engraved; and even a spoon-warmer in the shape of a cockleshell. The chafing-dish, with ebony mounts, sometimes has its little stand, as does the small brandy warmer.

Gadrooning

A term which is worth remembering, for the form of decoration it signifies appears on furniture, ceramics, and metal of all sorts, and in all ages. The Elizabethans loved it for those bulbous or 'melon' table legs of theirs (see pp. 72 and 73), which if you bought your 'refectory' table in the 1930's you may find you have too.

I suppose you would describe it as convex or concave fluting, meeting at the ends.

A most desirable form of decoration for a delftware (*v. Looking in Junk Shops*) plate or dish, as you will see on referring to the Lambeth plate shown under NEVERS.

Gallé

You will not find the work of Emile Gallé (1846–1904) very cheaply nowadays; on the other hand, it is not particularly dear for what it is. In fact, here you have one of those items which dealers put a price on in the hope of interesting a collector, but have to wait sometimes before he turns up.

This may very well be because nowadays we are not so enamoured of all those decorative forms of flowers and other plants, fishes, animals, seashells, and the cloudy, dreamy effects beloved of those who romantically yearned after nature at the end of the nineteenth century.

But some of these pieces are superb examples of glassmaking skill. Gallé used every trick in the book, and a lot more of his own devising – crazing and crackling, repeated 'flashings' in different colours, cutting and carving in relief, etching and engraving. You can see the influence of Japan in his work, also the 'back to nature' movement, ART NOUVEAU, even the Pre-Raphaelite movement. In Paris the value of Gallé glass has tripled in two years.

Gallé glass vase and signature

The best work was done in Gallé's own lifetime and this usually bears his scrawled signature, together with the place-name, 'Nancy' or 'Deposé' or perhaps the initials 'G.G.' The work carried on after his death, more or less on factory lines, lacking the touch of the master – although it can still be very acceptable for the likes of you and me – usually bears the name of 'Gallé' only.

If you get interested in a school of glassmaking in which France made a notable comeback after several undistinguished centuries, look also for the work of Joseph Brocard, Eugène Rousseau, Daum of Nancy, and a firm which marked its wares 'La Verrerie Française'.

Garniture de Cheminée

In spite of all the removals and smashings of the years one regularly sees at sales examples of the *garniture de cheminée*; in other words, the chimney-piece set. (Cf. the 'garnish' of pewter platters, dishes and saucers, a dozen of each, kept on the livery CUP BORDES by our ancestors.)

What splendid affairs these looked, if we had an impressive enough mantelpiece! Most often seen perhaps is the set of porcelain vases and beakers, sometimes three in number, but more augustly five. Arranged on brackets in steps, or standing like soldiers in a row, the three vases and two beakers not only presented their front view but also their back, by reflection in the mirror behind. As well as the fine Chinese ones, in blue and white, which were enormously popular here for two centuries, there were those in the various FAMILLE styles, made by our own Bow, Worcester, Chelsea, and other factories. Many of these *garnitures*, it is sad to reflect, may have been

Garniture de cheminée of Chinese blue and white porcelain

split up either by breakage or by dispersal among daughters. Full Chinese porcelain *garnitures* must have come here all through the nineteenth century, to judge by the number left: but the English potters seem to have decided by 1851 to cater for smaller chimney-pieces, for the catalogues offer *garnitures* of only three pieces.

It is thought that the *garniture* may have been suggested by the Chinese bronze altar set of incense burner, pair of candlesticks, and pair of vases. This does seem closely related to another sort of eighteenth-century *garniture*, which comprises a clock, a pair of candelabra, and a pair of covered urns.

German Silver

There is silver from Germany, but this is not the same as *German Silver*, which is not silver at all, but an alloy of copper, zinc and nickel. In fact it is pretty nearly the same as TOOTH AND EGG, which, as explained under that heading, is not Tutenag, but Paktong. The Italians correctly called it *Pacfong*, the French *Maillechort* (after the first makers in Paris, M. Maille and M. Chort), and the Germans *Neusilber*. Others called it *Argentan*.

As for us we have called it BRITISH PLATE under which name it is described; and it is basically what we use for our ELECTRO-PLATE.

Ginger Jars

There is one kind of Ginger Jar, with 'cracked ice' blue and white decoration which has already been covered in *Looking in Junk Shops*, but there is also another. This is of a much coarser ware, usually with the neck left unglazed, and decorated under the glaze with scenes in the broad summary brush strokes which hark back to the very earliest days of Chinese pottery.

These jars tell the story of three fishermen brothers, one a hunchback who fished only by the shore with a rod and line. The other two put to sea in their junk, which you see with a great question mark above it, the sign of an approaching typhoon. Apparently they never returned, for on the shore is their shuttered cabin; their hunchback brother stands alone casting his line, waiting eternally for his lost brothers.

One of the delights of collecting is the way you can find an ordinary commercial grocery container telling a story, like Keats with his Grecian urn.

'Three brothers' ginger jar

Gothic

This word has been thrown at the reader pretty often, and an explanation is due. Without going into probable origins in Romanesque and Byzantine (I have seen echoes of both in the junk shops) let us call Gothic that flowering of primarily Northern feeling towards spirituality which expressed itself in the most intricate, lovely, delicate forms, but as a kind of engineering in stone. Outstanding feature, of course, is the pointed arch.

Gothic furniture, what there was of it, except for woodwork in the churches, is therefore really beside the point. But Gothic affects our junk shop gazing in two forms, or perhaps three: the 'amusing' Gothick of Chippendale and Horace Walpole and even the Windsor chair (v. *Looking in Junk Shops*); the 'Romantic' Gothic of the 'Abbotsford' CHAIR (see page 47); and the 'holy' Gothic which gave us all those Betjeman churches. These two last are mentioned under VICTORIAN STYLES.

Gourd

One of the most frequently seen shapes in pottery and metal is that which looks like a tightly-laced Victorian lady without a head. It is called the gourd-shape, a term which long puzzled me, for the gourd is a round fruit sometimes with a long neck, with no such tight lacing as is shown in the bottles.

Then I realised that if you hollowed out a GOURD or calabash, tied a string round the neck, and dried the shell hard, you had an excellently handy bottle.

The shape given by this simple primitive device attracted the attention of potters and metal workers of ancient Persia, India and China, was copied by the Dutch delftware makers, and has come right down to

18th-century gourd-shaped Canton enamel vase

Victorian bone china. Doubtless somebody is making the shape today without in the least knowing why.

Greybeards
Another name for BELLARMINES, after the bearded masks which appear on the necks of these stoneware jugs.

Halberds and Partisans
Enthusiasts for swords and daggers are seldom to be seduced from their main obsession, which makes it a little easier for the rest of us to buy all those staff weapons or pole-arms with such other-worldly names, and at the same time such realistic properties in the way of cutting, slashing, chopping and poking. And, strangely enough, decorating.

There is the halberd, with its axe blade and lance point, and the partisan – a simple long-handled axe. There are lances, rawcons, spontoons, glaives and bills, whose shapes I will leave you the pleasure of discovering for yourself. There is also the battle-axe family: I saw one of those rather unsporting Indian ones having a dagger concealed in the handle, together with four other European ones, for only seventy-five pounds recently; and I feel sure an insurance company would make quite a substantial reduction on your burglary premium if you had those five weapons in your hall, together with five fine sons to wield them.

15th/16th-century English bill

The idea may outrage serious collectors, but for me these staff weapons have the same sort of decorative appeal as farm and other OLD IMPLEMENTS, a thought which I have developed under that head. Not all of them are as dear as the battle axes. Unless they have some specially interesting or costly metal work they can often be found for ten pounds or so apiece. I saw for twenty pounds, the other day, a 'lot' consisting of a fork, and six very serviceable spontoons with diagonally curved blades. I think it could be a rewarding thing to buy a 'lot' of this sort and watch one's guests trying not to notice.

Horn Ware
You will often come across horn drinking cups, but not so often, perhaps, those with engraving on them: this was an art practised more often abroad than here.

But there are also horn snuff boxes, often inlaid with silver, like the hair ornaments which really come under the heading of JEWELLERY. Horn buttons pressed with reliefs are sometimes found; also cane handles of animal heads, the eyes being put in with white opaque glass. Knives and forks are found with horn handles – and of course the oldest 'lanthorns' have horn windows and old horn books, or children's school books, had horn covers. A homely art, but one that brings you close to the daily life of people a long time ago.

There are also the horns you blow: these are treasured relics in many countries, often richly mounted, and capable of making a very loud noise indeed.

Hundred Antiques

This is a famous pattern found not only on Chinese porcelain, but also on the work of English factories which took it up, especially Worcester. Officially it is called *Po-ku*. The word 'hundred' here means 'many' rather than a literal number. It refers to the many different symbols brought into the pattern, signifying much respected items in the expressive language of Chinese symbolism. They include the Four Accomplishments, the Four Treasures of the Room of Literature, and various other objects including usually the Eight Precious Things. These comprise the Sonorous Stone, a bell which is a symbol of good judgment; the Pair of Books, which is an emblem of learning and constitutes a CHARM against evil spirits; the pair of Rhinoceros Horns, carved as drinking cups which signify happiness; the Artemisia leaf for curing illness; the Pearl, which stands for feminine purity and beauty and also wards off fires, floods and tempests;

The Eight Precious Things

Top: the Pearl; the Coin. *2nd line:* the Painting or Mirror;
the Lozenge. *3rd line:* the Sonorous Stone; the Pair of Books.
Bottom: the Rhinoceros Horns; the Artemisia Leaf

the Coin, denoting wealth; the Painting or Mirror, signifying married bliss; and the Lozenge or ancient musical instrument, for victory. In the patterns these symbols have down the ages become somewhat stylised, so we offer some sketches to help in identifying them.

Hundred Children

If you are about to be married and wish to be sure that you have many children, it will be useful if among your wedding presents there is a piece of porcelain bearing the pattern of the *Shua Wa Wa*, or the Hundred Playing Boys. This does not mean that you will actually get a round century of them, for in this usage, as in the HUNDRED ANTIQUES, the numeral really means just 'many'.

The Hundred Children, as it is usually called – though all the characters seem to be boys – is a charming pattern, and shows lots of little Chinese imps playing their games, fighting, pulling a toy horse, throwing a ball, pulling each other along in carts, at hide-and-seek, flying kites, bathing each other, etc. I don't know that I've ever seen the pattern on English china or earthenware – a pity!

Hunting Jugs

These very fine examples of BROWNWARE or saltglazed brown stoneware will be recognised by their graceful shapes, their deep reliefs of game and hunting scenes round the sides, and the beautifully modelled handle in the form of a greyhound. At least, it is in one version: there is another in which the hound is a mere rudimentary outline and the jug the typical Doulton or Brampton shape with a pinched-in spout. These are sometimes called 'dog-handled' jugs.

Hunting jug

Presumably the first was your fine presentation piece for the kitchen dresser, the second for thumping upon an inn table. There are mugs to match (see page 38).

Apart from the factories and marks mentioned under BROWNWARE, there are jugs to be found which are impressed on the bottom with 'S. & G.' and which were once attributed to Shore and Goulding, Isleworth, Middlesex. It is now known, however, that these were made by a firm called Schiller & Gerbing, potters working at Tetschen, Bohemia. The mark was made in all honesty, so here is a case of collectors deceiving themselves rather than being deceived by others.

Indian Tree

This famous design, still being produced today after a century and a half, is nearly as old as the Willow Pattern (*v. Looking in Junk Shops*), and in fact has family connections with it. The Caughley factory, where the Willow Pattern was produced by Thomas Turner about 1870, was bought by a former apprentice named John Rose, who already owned Coalport; and the Indian Tree pattern came out in 1801, at a time when wares were being potted at Caughley

Indian tree pattern

and sent to Coalport for decoration. Obviously based on a Chinese FAMILLE ROSE original, it picked up its name because in those times, when most oriental porcelain came here in the ships of the East India Companies, 'India' stood for 'China' as well. In its early days it was printed from copper plates and then coloured in by hand: today it will probably have been put on by lithography. The date of your 'Indian Tree' piece is therefore to be discovered only by reference to its material, its marks – if any – and the method of decorating.

Italian Comedy

Those who like to rub their noses against the windows of glass cases in museums, or prowl around the big auction rooms from time to time, will have come across a family of porcelain figures seeming to represent energetic and graceful movement suddenly frozen, as with an instantaneous photograph. There are the figures of Columbine, Harlequin and Pierrot, familiar from our own pantomime, as well as other characters such as the Doctor, Pantaloon, the swaggering Captain, Scaramouche, and Mezzotino.

Porcelain figure of Harlequin from Italian Comedy

These gay and lively folk are from the *Commedia dell'Arte*, or Italian Comedy, an entertainment which entranced the whole of Europe in the seventeenth century. To judge by the taste of it given us a few years ago by the Piccolo Scala, from Milan, it was an exquisite combination of mime, song, dance, and wonderful clowning, mostly improvised around outrageous themes of lovers' intrigues, old men's foolishness, woman's inconstancy, man's braggadocio, and the eventual triumph of the servant and his Dulcinella.

Chelsea and Bow were in time to make these figures, but by the end of the eighteenth century we had to make do with Wedgwood's busts of classical authors and Staffordshire's endless dogs.

Jacobean

For most of us this means oak gate-leg tables and barley-sugar turning. But this is perhaps a little premature. The heyday of barley-sugar was in Restoration times.

Early Jacobean (say 1600–1650) gave us a lighter, more restrained version of Elizabethan, cf. the modified 'melons' shown on page 72. The severe lines of our dining table show how far this had gone by the time Cromwell became Lord Protector.

H

Jacobean dining table

Neo-Jacobean, if that is what one calls it, came in about the twenties of this century, and gave us 'refectory' and gate-leg TABLES all over again, either in dark or fumed oak. What was well enough made to survive is in use or in the junk shops, but you can also still buy it new.

Japanese Sword Fittings

At sales there sometimes turn up collections of small metal objects most superbly worked with chasing, embossing, inlaying, DAMASCENING. They are the various fittings belonging to the Japanese sword; and although they vary a lot in price, if you like beautiful workmanship in metal here is one of the cheapest and most convenient ways of putting together a fine collection.

Outstanding is the round or oval flat piece of metal, pierced with a large slit and two smaller holes – the *Tsuba* or sword guard, mounted where handle meets blade. Many of them, the older pieces, are in hammered iron with silver inlay, and they show such subjects as wild geese flying, dragons, and serpents, crayfish, plum trees in copper with silver blossoms, figures of sages and beauties, landscapes like those in coloured prints, and so on. Much use was made for decoration of beautiful soft alloys like *shakudo*, a combination of bronze and gold, and *shibuchi*, bronze and silver, both of which can acquire a PATINA.

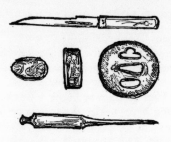

Japanese sword fittings (*enlarged*)

The two holes on either side of the sword hole were for the *kodzuka*, a small dagger which fitted on to one side of the sheath; and the *kogai*, a kind of stiletto or skewer, which was housed on the other side. They must have made a very handy set of tools in an emergency, but like the swords themselves, they are not very cheap nowadays: more accessible are the other small fittings, like the *menukis*, or tiny plates of metal on the grip of the hilt; the *kachira*, a metal cap on the top of the hilt, and the *fuchi*, a ring of metal resting on the *tsuba*. Both *kachira* and *fuchi* were often made by the same man, so you get *fuchikachira*. Even in these small things you can discover tigers in bamboo thickets, silver bats, battle scenes, and landscapes with golden moons.

As I say, prices vary, from perhaps a pound a piece up to high prices for the finest work. The later ones, made especially for the tourist trade rather than for swords, betray themselves by flashy workmanship; but the earlier sort are worthy of anyone's attention.

Japanese sword

Japanesque

I use this word to describe, not the products of Japan, or even those things specially made for the export trade to Europe – so very different from many of the things she likes to keep at home – but rather for the articles made here 'under the influence' as it were.

Somewhere in the eighteen sixties, soon after Commodore Perry had appeared with his warships in Nagasaki harbour and provided the circumstances for the plot of *Madame Butterfly*, Europe suddenly found itself enraptured by Japanese art. It was due for another craze of this sort, having by now forgotten the *Chinoiseries* (*v. Looking in Junk Shops*) of the eighteenth century. Manet and Whistler fell under the spell, not only of the asymmetrical designs but also of Chinese blue and white porcelain (*v. Looking in Junk Shops*), and it is really the mixture of these two quite different forms of art, with a very generous helping of VICTORIAN STYLE, which went to make up the Japanesque.

Worcester moved in very quickly with PILGRIM BOTTLES, jugs and other items in 'ivory porcelain' decorated with 'Japanese' figures in relief, so did Doulton, Wedgwood and others. You can see the same feeling in lots of things left by the smaller potteries,

'Japanesque' chair, c. 1880

with decorations of fishes, seaweed, grasses and the
like. The Watcombe, Linthorpe, Elton potteries, and
the Martin brothers went Japanesque at some time
or another. All this led quite simply to BAMBOO
furniture, Japanese painted screens, sideboards and
overmantels and hallstands in Japanned wood with
perforated panels, and some little 'occasional' tables
with splayed legs and fretted panels in the sides.

These were pretty fragile, much more so than the
bamboo, so any still surviving must have had tender
treatment over the last eighty years or so.

Jewellery

If we are going to look for jewellery, either in the junk
shops or on the market stalls, we should perhaps make
up our minds from the beginning that we are not
likely to find anything which is *intrinsically* valuable,
that is, made up of precious stones or metals. All these

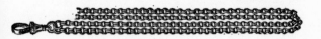

Victorian lorgnette or muff chains
(a) Prince of Wales pattern (b) Alma pattern (c) Trace pattern

places are combed regularly by eagle-eyed dealers and such pieces soon find their level in the more expensive shops where a large overhead for plush carpets and bright lights is immediately added to their price.

But if we have an eye and a taste for workmanship, for the commonly overlooked qualities of the semi-precious gemstones – like the deep purple or lilac amethyst, the yellowish or bottle-green peridot, the deep-red or green garnet, the pale blue aquamarine, the reddish carnelian; if we are bored with the jeweller's shop windows which are full of all the standard jewellery stuck about with miserable little diamond chips ('We *must* have a diamond ring, mustn't we?'), then here is where a pound or two can buy you a lot of fun, even if it takes up a lot of your time.

Our first choice will be among pieces which have either been set in pinchbeck, and other cheap materials such as copper, bronze, even steel and iron: or which make the most sparing use of gold, as with filigree work, early ELECTRO gilding, plated gold and silver (what we would call 'rolled'). Some fine artistry went into the stick pins, brooches, rings, bracelets, pendants, lockets, etc., made in this way as substitutes for precious metals, and we shall be wise in our generation if we look very hard at things which happen to be out of fashion at the moment: they will certainly come in again, as all things do. Sporting brooches and pins, especially those in fifteen carat gold with pearl daisies, turquoise horseshoes and hearts, 'merry-thoughts' and the rest are plentiful. The double moon, wheat ears and flight of swallows can be found, also little baskets with flowers of jewels.

There were once many, many chains on dresses for

Victorian gold horseshoe bracelet and curb chain
bracelet in gold

attachment of lorgnettes, muffs, or chatelaines, and
some of these are still about for the finding, anything up to fifty-four inches long, in 'trace', 'curb',
'alma', or 'Prince of Wales' pattern. There is the
occasional chatelaine for holding charms in the shape
of pigs, shoes, 'tee-to-tum', spinners, acorns, lucky
stars. The late Victorian motor car, if made now,
would appear as a 'veteran', but then as the very latest
in transport. Old-fashioned men's jewellery is about,
too, not only as cuff-links, tiepins and rings, but as
'Alberts', or short chains worn dangling from the
watch-chain, with pendants perhaps in the form of a
fancy padlock, a seal, a compass, or a locket containing
a miniature photograph.

Look also for flies under crystal (or 'lead glass' as
it is more likely to be), also ear-rings in the shape of
hammers, tongs, or ladders. The Victorians liked
'folk' jewellery when it was shown to them in exhibi-
tions – the 'Scotch' silver brooches of claymores and
shields set with cairngorms, or 'Scotch Topaz', are
still about, also pieces modelled on ancient Irish
brooches. Hair jewellery is sought nowadays by collectors, either actual things made of twisted hair, or
as little glass boxes or lockets, carrying a pathetic
lock of hair which has never aged. There is mourning
jewellery in jet which is sometimes very handsome
and beautifully worked. There is fine carving in coral,
as in ivory, particularly of animals against mountain
scenery.

Gold chain brooch and gilt wishbone brooch

A few other items to look for: marcasite, first popular in Georgian times, is really only iron pyrites, one of the commonest of metals. It has been made into beautiful things by cutting and faceting, especially as a frame for coloured stones and enamels: these are best when they are pavé set, the turned-over edges of the mount adding light to the stone. Cut-steel, similar in appearance to marcasite, was another eighteenth-century craze, as we know from the many Wedgwood cameos mounted on it; but whereas in their early days each steel head was individually set, the invention of die-stamping gave us cut-steel jewellery in ribbons and so brought it down the scale and it was no longer used for the better stones.

The poker-about-in-trays should not overlook amber pieces, ivory, and enamelling. Large enamelled jewellery is out of fashion, but it will probably never be made again except by amateurs.

Finally, one could recommend a search for pieces made at the turn of the century by craftsmen working under the influence first of the Arts and Crafts movement led by William Morris, then in the styles of ART NOUVEAU. French designers headed by the Réné LALIQUE of glass fame, broke away completely from the conventional diamond-set jewellery and made lovely things in such materials as horn, black and coloured enamel, ivory, mother-of-pearl, as well as in the more precious metals. Instead of using stones for their intrinsic value, they very properly considered only their decorative value, seeking out unusual, though not very precious, metals like Mexican or Fire opals,

malachite and azurite, Connemara marble or serpentine, the light green amazonite and the pearl
'blisters' scorned by the seekers after cash values. They
also did some fine enamelling. The big names in the
movement were C. R. Ashbee who worked a great
deal in dull polished silver with a sparing use of gemstones; the Gaskins, husband and wife, produced some
fine work in twisted wire; and others made attractive
brooches, clasps, pendants and pins, with much
fine wrought and beaten work in silver, aluminium
and copper.

As to types of setting, I suppose everyone knows
that a *Claw* setting is one in which the stone is held
by little 'claws' of metal, while with *Carved* settings
the stone is bedded in solid metal. *Millegrain* leaves the
back open and holds the stone with little raised grains
of the metal; *Pavé* set stones are close together held by
little points of metal; and *Cabochon* stones could be set
in a box whose edges grasp the stone, the back being
cut away to allow the light to show through.

Not many people realise how interesting it can be
to put together a collection of gemstones simply *as*
stones rather than as decoration in jewellery. They
can be bought, either in old and worthless settings or
direct from a lapidary – that is to say, a specialist in
stones – at a fairly modest cost. If that sounds surprising it should be remembered that the bulk of the
price of most jewellery sold in the shops rests upon
the labour put into the mount, as well as the
thick carpets, the exquisite salesfolk and purchase
tax.

A gathering of stones will teach you a lot about their
qualities. To take semi-precious stones alone, you can
get to know the striped agate and onyx, the colour-
changing alexandrite, the blood-stone – with its red

Art nouveau jewellery

drops in a sea of chalcedony – the brown zircon, the green and red tourmaline, the sherry-brown, blue or pink topaz, the russet-red sard, the many-coloured spinel, the golden amber, the black jet, the jasper disguising itself as lapis lazuli. By handling and comparing these very cheaply acquired stones, you can get to know a great deal about their *Hue*, which means how much actual colour they have: their *Tone*, otherwise their lightness and darkness: their *Intensity*, or vividness. Since there are hundreds of *Hues*, and thousands of *Tones*, this should keep you going for some little time. Then, with some stones, one is interested in their *Lustre*, or *Texture* – whether it is silky, pearly, waxy, or glassy etc. Their *Translucency*, as in moonstones, is of interest, also their *Transparency*, as in aquamarines. Stones which come in different colours and therefore baffle on that account can be identified by a scale of hardness based on the extent to which one sort of stone will scratch a mark on another.

You measure your stones by the carat, which is two-tenths of a grain. Two other points – if you are going to gather these stones don't let them rub together, for the hard ones will scratch the soft ones: and keep them clean and free from dusty air with a non-greasy detergent. Mount them, for preference, in a silk lined box with a window.

Nobody can talk about gemstones for long without bringing in birthdays. January's garnet ensures that your lover will be faithful to you: February's stone is the amethyst, which according to a rather scandalous legend about Bacchus and a frightened nymph, keeps you sober. In March you have the choice of aquamarine, which gives you courage and energy, or bloodstone by which you acquire great wisdom. April folk are a lucky lot, for they have the diamond which ensures victory in any enterprise: while May has the emerald, which ensures women wedded bliss and safe child-bearing. June's children have the moonstone which banishes nightmares, and the pearl which makes all brides beautiful. July's ruby frees you from worldly cares: in August the peridot, or evening emerald, makes you merciful to others: September's sapphire stands for truth and sincerity. October has the opal, no longer considered unlucky, and the tourmaline, which since it becomes electrified by a change in atmosphere is said to be as good as a glass of champagne to its rightful wearer. November's topaz cures sleeplessness, and in December the turquoise brings both love and money and lapis lazuli cures melancholy. So everything seems to have been worked out for everybody in the nicest possible way.

Kauffmann

You will doubtless have come across prints after Angelica Kauffmann's pictures, engraved by BARTOLOZZI and others: and will also have seen them reproduced on china and furniture. Born in 1741 in Switzerland, she made a name for painting in Rome, and then came to London, where she stayed for about fifteen years, painting portraits and also the decorative historical and classical pictures for which she is chiefly known. The author of *Nollekens and his Times* tells a couple of stories about her, one of which is that she married a servant under the mistaken impression he was a count: the marriage was dissolved after a suitable financial arrangement.

Prints like 'Cupid bound to a Tree by Nymphs', 'Venus Presenting Helen to Paris', 'Beauty Cornered by Love', became famous, and are still sought after in their early states. Many of these prints came in circular or oval form and have been so framed.

Besides BARTOLOZZI, Angelica Kauffmann was engraved by W. W. Ryland, Thomas Burke, Thomas Cheesman, in fact most of the leading stipple engravers of the day. She eventually returned to Rome, and died in 1807.

Knife Rests

There are some small underconsidered items which have been made in all sorts of materials from the cheapest to the dearest; and they are the very stuff of junk shop collecting. Among them are the aids to the family carver known as knife rests. Upon these he rested his carving implements while he hastily snatched a few mouthfuls before his sons came back for another helping.

Usually in pairs, they are to be found in porcelain, glass and various sorts of metals: I even seem to remember a pair in Bilston enamel. Sometimes they take the form of short rails with legs at each end surmounted by some sort of device: others are in the form of flat circle segments with raised sides.

Nobody, I suppose, would ever claim great beauty for them, although Victorian silver ones exist which have been given as much consideration by the designer as anything else on the table. But for those who have to watch their shillings here is a field in which they can line up with the expert, especially in the realm of porcelain. Buyers of more splendid things can fall back upon a factory mark, but as these little things seldom bear such signposts your knife-rest collector will benefit from having to learn his connoisseurship the hard way.

Lace Bobbins

Many people like to look for these attractive and highly individual little bobbins used by the lace-makers on their pillows.

What makes them interesting to collect is that they are all different: this in fact was the very point of them, for as the lacemaker worked the design she had to select each bobbin separately. Many of them are dated, and some bear the owner's name or initials.

I suppose most of those one sees nowadays are of bone, ivory or wood, but they are also to be found in brass, pewter, even silver and gold. But it is those in the more humble wood that are the most charming; they evidently, as often as not, originated as tender offerings to a girl with a lace-making pillow from a chap with a handy knife.

'Let me have the wedding day, dear' has been noted, also the rather forward 'Meet me by moonlight alone'. One also sees 'Sweet love, be mine', and 'Kiss me quick, and don't be shy'.

Some bobbins have puzzling inscriptions on them which were evidently some sort of code; or they are about some event like a battle or the Jubilee. Collectors are particularly keen, however, on those that give

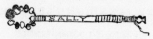

Bone and bead lace bobbin

a hint of the district of origin, whether it be Bucking-
hamshire, Bedfordshire, Oxfordshire or Northampton-
shire – one important lace-making district – or over in
Devon and Wiltshire. You can also seek these things
abroad, for the lace-making craft was – and often still
is – carried on in Normandy, around Brussels, and in
Spain, Portugal and Italy.

Lalique

It was back in Edwardian days that we first met the
glass of Réné Lalique (1860–1945). To those of us
who lived in Mayfair or South Kensington it came
chiefly in the form of decorative bowls, figures for the
cabinet or mantelpiece, lamp stands, clocks and even
screens or panels for our furniture. Those of us who
lived elsewhere looked at it wistfully in Bond Street
windows in the form of scent bottles: and in fact
Lalique did actually, as a supplier to Coty, revolu-
tionise the scent-bottle industry, so he has to be
brought into any collection of them. Did you throw
all yours away?

Lalique started life as a goldsmith, and when he
turned to glassmaking he broke away from the
coloured and enamelled glass with which everyone
was obsessed, and went in search of what M. Barrelet
called a 'harmony of whites'. Using a pure colourless
glass, he moulded, pressed and engraved, getting his
best effects with a combination of clear and white mat
surfaces. He also produced an interesting range of
opaque black glass. He was one of the few artists who
managed to produce his work on a factory scale. His
son, Marc Lalique, continues the good work.

You may also be interested in the work of another Frenchman who helped in the revival of glassmaking in his country, viz. Emile GALLÉ.

Lancastrian Pottery

One by one the late Victorian potteries re-establish themselves, and come forward to be collected. The best of the Royal Lancastrian lustre ware has been collected for many years now; in fact, being real hand-craft and artistry, it was collected almost as soon as it was offered for sale. But even quite modest pieces are now in that mezzanine or remove where the dealers recognise the factory mark and realise that although unfashionable at the moment and not to be given away to Aunt Agatha for ten shillings, a piece will make a couple of pounds when a collector turns up.

The Royal Lancastrian Pottery was founded by William Burton as an offshoot of the Pilkington tile and brick factory at Clifton, near Manchester. Burton was one of those geniuses, like Wedgwood, Spode and Minton, one often finds in ceramics – part chemist, part artist, part business man. In the early years he produced some of the best of the wonderful coloured glazes which rivalled those of Chinese porcelain. Some were in monochrome, some had variegated colours, and there were fascinating textures as well. With the work of Bernard MOORE and William MOORCROFT and others, they marked a new era in English pottery.

Next came the famous Pilkington iridescent lustre. This differs from most lustre in that the effect is of the changing colours on a soap bubble, and the decorators employed under Gordon M. Forsyth, the art director, began to produce with its aid that fine series of painted wares in which classical, Spanish,

Persian, Italian and ART NOUVEAU themes were somehow pulled together into what is now beginning to
have a very definite character of its own. The third
main class of pottery was what the firm called Lapis
Ware, an original kind of stoneware in which the
painting combined with or reacted against the glaze
put on over it in such a way as to produce effects of
mottled or speckled flowing colour on tinted grounds.

Lancastrian ware of any kind was never very cheap,
and it fell a victim to the industrial depression: Pilkington stopped making art pottery in about 1938.

Except for some of the early glazed pieces made
before 1904, Lancastrian is easy to trace not only to
the factory, but to the artist, and even sometimes to
its year of production. Painters like W. S. Mycock,
Gwladys Rogers, Richard Joyce, and designers like
Walter Crane and Lewis F. Day had their special
monograms in addition to the firm's 'PL' with two
bees (for the brothers Burton). There were also numbers beginning at 2001 in 1905.

Some Lancastrian ware I have seen looks rather
dulled, as though the glaze has not stood up to heat
or washing: but the best of it is really fine stuff and
worth looking for.

Latten

Latten is brass, but in a particular form. Before brass
was founded in this country (what the Elizabethans
called 'brass' was really bronze) it was brought here
from Germany and the Netherlands in flat sheets.
From these were made the brasses in our churches,
after which rubbings are taken. When we applied
the word 'brass' to describe what we had once called
bronze, the word 'latten' remained to describe brass
when it came in flat sheets rather than solid lumps.

Early horse brasses were made of latten, but this was made here, the alloy being copper and calamine instead of the later copper and zinc. They should show the hammer marks on the back. Early brass kettles, skillets, measures and other pots were also hammered out of latten brass.

Latticinio

Threads of white opaque or coloured glass, sometimes in slender spirals, sometimes in broad loops, is a form of decoration which glass-makers have been using since the times of ancient Egypt.

Today you see it mostly in the sort of glass made at Nailsea (*v. Looking in Junk Shops*) and elsewhere, especially in Birmingham and Stourbridge. John Northwood, famous for his CAMEO GLASS, invented a special 'pulling up' machine which would do mechanically what the glassblowers had for centuries been doing by hand: that is, winding threads of glass round a mould, blowing the vessel into it, then combing down the loops.

In its more aristocratic forms from Venice, whether in European FAÇON DE VENISE or in Stourbridge acts of homage to this whole school of glassmaking, the scholarly refer to this as *latticino, latticinio*, or *lattimo*, i.e. milk glass: when the threads are very fine indeed, and cross each other as in lace, this latter word appears, i.e. *vetro di trina*. France has a family of such glass: the last time I was in Paris I saw a most seductive little bottle in looped white, pale green and cobalt, which was priced at only about a pound.

Laughing Buddha

This is one of the most familiar figures in Chinese porcelain, a fat man squatting with his jacket open,

I

smiling happily and displaying a magnificent corporation. Strictly speaking he is not the Buddha at all, but *Pu T'ai Ho Shang*, a Boddhisattva (who needs one more life to attain Buddha-hood) and one of the Eighteen Lohans or Arhats, i.e. early disciples of the Buddha. Treat him with respect, for he represents Riches and Contentment.

Laughing buddha

Legs and Feet

Nobody can take an interest in furniture without getting involved in both the legs and feet below them. As it is a hopeless task trying to recognise them from descriptions, here are a few sketches. Perhaps the most famous and elaborate is the *Cabriole*, which turned up late in the seventeenth century much to the delight of the BAROQUE and ROCOCO designers. It is said to have been adapted from a goat's leg, the word in French signifying a goat's leap.

The most ubiquitous since about Jacobean times because of its cheapness in labour is the *Turned*, closely followed by the *Taper*, much favoured by Hepplewhite and Sheraton. The fluted *Pillar* legs were fashionable in the days of WILLIAM AND MARY. Another animal

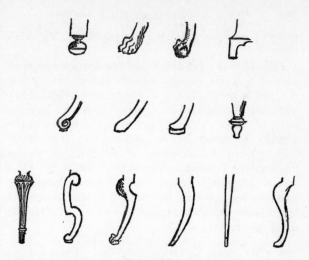

Feet and legs

Top: Bun; paw; claw and ball; bracket. *Middle:* Scroll; pad; club; turned. *Bottom:* Pillar; scroll; hock; sabre; taper; cabriole

form was the *Hock*, which describes itself, as do the *Sabre* and the *Scroll*.

For feet you could have the ordinary *Bracket*, the *Scroll* (or *Whorl*), the *Turned*, the *Ball*, the *Club* and the *Bun*. Animal forms crop up again in the *Paw*, the *Claw and Ball*, the *Hoof* and the *Pad*.

All these terms are fairly self-describing, but the artist will be more helpful than I.

Nothing is to be taken for granted in dating furniture, but by taking other things into consideration as well, the shapes of legs and feet can be quite helpful.

Lithophanes

Not very often met with nowadays – I suppose I have seen one in the last two years – are these 'shadow pictures' in china which were so popular in Victorian days.

Lithophanes were made by impressing a design or picture in a thin glassy porcelain in such a way that it could be seen only when held against a light. They were used for lampshades, night lights and in some parts of the country they are even to be seen in the windows of houses. For subjects the makers generally relied upon popular pictures of the day. Many were made on the Continent, especially in Berlin, but Mintons, Copelands, Wedgwoods, Graingers of Worcester and others also turned them out. The one I saw measured about ten inches by seven inches, but some are much larger than this.

A similar effect is to be seen in some Chinese porcelain dating back to Ming times, though the process here is an infinitely delicate carving with a fine point.

Locks and Keys

When you look at the average modern lock it is scarcely to be wondered at that joiners should have hidden them away in mortices. But old locks, if you can find them, are very different. They were meant not only to be seen but to impress people, and the metalworker really went to town on them. Gilded wrought iron, blue steel, LATTEN brass, Princes metal (a brass alloy), pinchbeck, were all brought into use, and enriched with moulding, engraving, DAMASCENING, with gold and silver on steel.

Though really fine old locks may be rarities, the old keys made to fit them are much more frequent visitors to the salerooms. These, too, are quite worth collecting – like JAPANESE SWORD FITTINGS – merely as fine and very beautiful metalwork. They were important and treasured articles of use in their day,

17th-century key and locks

and each one was given a well-designed 'bow' – the part you hold to turn it in the lock. Crosses, flying cherubs, figures of saints, winged griffins, coronets were among the motifs used. In a recent sale I saw a group of Roman keys sold for very little: and if it surprises you to hear that the Romans *had* keys, let alone locks to put them in, I read recently that even the Ancient Britons had locks, wooden ones which they bought from the Phoenicians. I did not know they had doors even.

Louis XIV, XV, XVI

Junk-shop haunters will sometimes find the names of these French kings hurled at them with terrific assurance. But the speaker will usually be referring not to the products of their reigns but to the imitations manufactured both in England and in France in Victorian days.

The French versions are fairly faithful to their originals: but the English ones never quite escape that transmogrification of the notions of other people and other times which makes nonsense of the claim that there is no such thing as a VICTORIAN STYLE. However, this does not seem to prevent such pieces being shipped across to France almost daily, working

Louis XIV armchair and Louis XV 'Marquise' chair 1 4

their way upwards from the shops around the Gare Montparnasse.

Since this is a tasting book rather than a text book one might roughly equate the styles of Louis XIV (1643–1715), Louis XV (1715–1774) and Louis XVI (1774–1793) with, respectively, BAROQUE magnificence, ROCOCO frivolity, and NEO-CLASSICAL ADAM austerity, all of which have their expressions in English.

Only we must bear in mind that French handling of a style is usually 'more so' – more magnificent, more

Louis XVI armchair

frivolous, more austere, as the case may be: the Cabriole LEG is a good example. As to relative dates, it is also as well to consider that anything French might be a generation in front of anything British.

Loving Cups

Nobody who has attended a public banquet will have escaped the ceremony of the loving cup. This large piece of silver plate, napkin tied to a handle, goes from guest to guest, each of whom remains standing while his neighbour drinks – in case someone has slipped into the Mansion House with a flick-knife and is looking for unwary drinkers.

A more intimate sort of loving cup comes in pottery of the main sorts, and is a small two-handled job for two friends having a quiet drink of toddy together. I have also heard them called 'parting cups', but as journeys end with lovers' meetings, so they must begin with lovers' partings.

Some loving cups had their owner's name or initials printed on them, or perhaps a name of a couple; others bore mottoes, and the arms of Societies such as the Oddfellows. A typical inscription is:

> *Cup love and friendship*
> *Peace and good neighbourhood*
> *May we never seen an ould friend*
> *with a new face*

All these have the values of the wares they are produced in, as well as any historical interest in the inscription, so you are not likely to find good ones at bargain prices. But there are later Victorian ones which are just as collectable; for example those in Chester-field BROWNWARE of the 1880s. Happily for the future of friendship, manufacture has not entirely died out: they are a speciality of the Rye pottery today in typical striped decoration.

Maps

Here is something which pleases both the collector and the decorator. Old maps with their griffins, dolphins, useful information about the whereabouts of cannibals and quicksands, cherubs puffing out their cheeks to blow favourable winds into the bellying sails of galleons, make splendid and sometimes very colourful pictures of which one does not soon tire. But as the early map-makers put in sea-fights, her-aldry and the rest – in other words included chaps in their maps – the student of history and geography also finds endless interest in them, especially if he carries on his study to its logical conclusion, that is to say, air, geological and other maps and charts.

Cheaply priced coloured maps one sees in the shops are, of course, modern reprints of the old ones. They

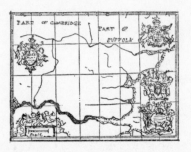

18th-century map

are well enough in their way, but a genuine old one, with its special quality of paper, printing and colouring, will effectively kill any reprints put alongside it.

Most famous of the early cartographers was Christopher Saxton (d. 1596), followed by John Norden and John Speed, all of whom are very collectable – though good examples are scarce. Maps by Robert Morden, which appeared about 1695, are keenly sought, and so is John Rocque's two-inch-to-the-mile map of Surrey and Sussex, which shows every house, garden and wood which existed there in 1762. The interesting county maps by the Bowens about 1770 give facts about the natural products and industries of the districts. Later ones give the canal and early railway systems, after which come the first Ordnance Survey maps.

Charts, of course, are just as fascinating, and if you are an armchair traveller you should one day treat yourself to a few old volumes of the *Admiralty Pilot*, which not only gives you a look at the coastline you are approaching, but information about the natives and amenities ashore.

Medals and Medallions

One tends to think of medals as synonymous only with the 'gongs' which tend to get pinned on one during wars, or sent in the post afterwards, together with the

Medal commemorating sea battle

grateful thanks of the Sovereign. There are, of course, collectors of these, and there is a tariff for fine examples all the way, historically, from the Victoria Cross to the George Medal.

Of more aesthetic and historic interest, I think, are the other sort of medal, struck to commemorate events, to celebrate the existence of great persons, or, on the other hand, to jeer at those persons. There were Coronation medals in many reigns, that of William IV being especially esteemed. Popes and kings struck medals to celebrate victories, or as political manifestos to make claims of one sort or another: Henry VIII put his claim to be head of the English Church on a medal, and Charles I warned all other powers by means of a medal that the Armada victory (itself celebrated on a coin) had made us top sea nation and that we intended to keep things that way. The seventeenth century was a great period for medals of this sort, the Dutch being just as eager to celebrate their victories as we were; while the Germans produced some fine ones as well. There are also other medals marking events in the history of the railways and flying, as well as talismanic or devotional medals.

Medallions are really only larger versions of medals: and the term is also used for panels or enclosures on other objects: neither coins, which are used for currency, nor PLAQUETTES, which are for purely aesthetic pleasure, are really in this field.

Memento Mori

This is a sales cataloguer's term for all those sad things which we once bought to remind ourselves of the dead – and of death.

There are RINGS, with a ribbon tie of hair in a bezel; there are lockets of all sorts also to contain hair curls, perhaps tied as a sheaf of corn; there are bracelets, wrist ornaments, pendants. There are also grim little items in which the principal decoration is a skull: the object here seems to be not to lament someone lost as to remind the wearer of his own mortality.

Mourning ring with skull

Moorcroft

The dashing signature of William Moorcroft (1871–1945) on the bottom of a vase is a sure sign of excellence and collectability in pottery. He was one of the pioneers in that group of potters in the late nineteenth century who worked out the secrets of the old Chinese porcelain glazes and expressed them on English earthenware. Perhaps his most distinctive wares are those in POWDER BLUE monochrome glazes and those where the decoration, usually of fruit and leaves, has a raised outline: a famous pattern has golden brown fruit and leaves against a deep blue background.

He produced FLAMBÉ and other glazes as well, and of all his work only a series of white vases with pale decoration has left me unenthralled. Moorcrofts are still flourishing today.

Moore (Bernard)

If you come across a piece of pottery having a beautiful rich coloured glaze, and impressed on the bottom with the name of Bernard Moore (1853–1935), you will have an example of the work of one of the English pioneers in re-creating the fine glazes used on Chinese porcelain. He specialised in FLAMBÉ and SANG DE BOEUF, also Persian blue and crystalline glazes.

Similar work was done by William MOORCROFT, the Royal LANCASTRIAN POTTERY and Doultons.

Moradabad Ware

This is a name used by dealers to cover almost anything which doesn't seem to be BENARES. Properly speaking it covers articles of tinned brass made in such centres as Moradabad, Jaipur and Kashmir. In one of the styles, the *sada*, the design is chased in the tinning, showing up in the 'gold' of brass. In the other, the *siyah-kalam*, the designs follow the styles of the more precious enamelled wares. They are chased in the brass, and the depressions filled with black or coloured lac. There are plates, dishes, water jars, jugs in all the shapes mentioned under BENARES and BIDRI work, and lots and lots of tumblers and small measures. Some pieces have spiral patterns of tiny rosettes, others arabesque patterns like Arabic writing.

The simpler the design, usually, the older the work. Many modern pieces have synthetic colouring instead

Moradabad brass spice box

of the true lac, so it is usually best to go for the black or plain CHASING.

Morland

People who like a well-painted picture as well as those unashamedly fond of the sentimental and the picturesque come together in their admiration for the prints of George Morland (1763–1804). Like the old Dutch painters, Morland loved to show the ordinary folk of the day, with their children, cows and horses and pigs: and though he sometimes over-dramatised his subject, he produced pictures much more real and engaging than most of the artists appearing in the colour prints of the day – especially those by engravers like BARTOLOZZI.

Most of the Morland prints you see were engraved by his brother-in-law William Ward and by J. R. Smith, generally in mezzotint. His output was enormous and varied, for he led a prodigal, reckless life, and was always having to make up for time lost in conviviality, and to pay off debts incurred on horses and entertainment. Like many another good artist he never really grew out of schoolboy jokes, and loved to have children playing around his studio as he painted them. At a time when more prosperous animal painters went in for prize-winning bulls and horses, Morland preferred to paint broken-down farmhorses and pigs.

My favourites are the scenes outside country inns or in stables, showing the farmers and ostlers, the village children, and mob-capped women, the gypsies, the beggars – and all those pigs. Anyone who can make a good picture out of a pig is a good painter.

For guidance in buying Morland prints as distinct from modern reproductions – and there are some

tolerably good ones – it may be worth turning back
to BARTOLOZZI.

Musical Boxes

A few years ago, when a favourite country pub of
mine was overwhelmed by that combination of taste-
less wallpaper, hardboard and staring lights which one
ought to include under our styles as Brewery Director's Folly, since it is neither period nor contemporary
but just damned uncomfortable – when this awful
thing happened I thought to have seen the last of the
pub's beloved 'Polyphon Automatic Musical Instrument', one of whose brothers appears on this page.

For fifty years it had hung on the wall of the saloon
bar receiving pennies, in return clunking out music-
hall and operatic tunes from its perforated steel plates.
Now, in its place, were three unidentifiable china birds
flying diagonally across the wall in line ahead.

But only the other day I saw a 'Polyphon' in a very
modern and very comfortable espresso bar, so, like

'The Polyphon'

other former habitués of the saloon bar – and for the same sort of reasons – it seems that these old favourites are spending their declining years in more congenial surroundings. The proprietor of the espresso told me that, by making a delicate adjustment to the mechanism, the 'Polyphon' now earned threepence a go instead of a penny: so that in only a few months it had recovered the thirty pounds laid out by its new master.

The old polyphon and its cousins – there are many variations – have a very long ancestry. Musical boxes seem to have started life, naturally enough, among the watchmakers, first as mechanism whereby little airs could be played by watches, then as musical movements fitted into bottles, seals, snuffboxes, walking-stick handles, even watchkeys and other objects of that sort. I have never quite recovered from the shock I had when, dining in the house of a Socialist politician, I raised a fine cut-glass decanter which thereupon played the Eton Boating Song. I hear, too, that there are chairs in which the unmusical ought not to sit.

Ambitious collectors in this field go in for super musical boxes which are really automata. There are singing-bird boxes which spring at you and warble merrily; there are boxes with dancing dolls, monkey bandsmen, marching soldiers on a fort, and all kinds of figures which do many kinds of things for as long as you keep them wound up.

But if you are going in for musical boxes it seems to me that you ought to concentrate on the music. If an old player-piano addict, you can find 'forte-piano' boxes which play loudly and softly at will, having two combs manipulated by a revolving cylinder. There are others which have built-in flutes, to say nothing of drums and bells, whistles and castanets.

Neo-

This prefix gets shoved in front of almost anything, from Neolithic (New Stone Age) to NEO-CLASSICAL, which is explained below.

It is often very misleading, for although the literal meaning is 'new', it never means an exact revival or repetition of something, only a new movement inspired by the old one. It can stretch over a thousand years, or it can be a direct succession, like the Neo-impressionists who gave Impressionism a push in a different direction – in fact towards Post-Impressionism.

Today, anything 'Neo' seems to be a horror – look at our bankers' 'Neo-Georgian'! Will 'Contemporary' one day become 'Neo-Modern'?

Neo-Classical

There was a moment in England about the end of the fifteenth century, when people became bored with the mystical geometry of GOTHIC and looked right back over the centuries at the simple, serene harmonies of the classical styles of Ancient Greece and Rome. This was the Renaissance, and it gave us Elizabethan and Restoration, BAROQUE and ROCOCO.

About the middle of the eighteenth century, as a result of the excavations at Pompeii and elsewhere, we took another and much closer look at the classical styles. This time we got a good deal nearer to them: and the story is told under ADAM.

Nevers

This French faience factory is mentioned for the unique sort of decoration it inspired in our Lambeth

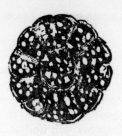

Early-18th-century Nevers-style
Lambeth delftware plate

delftware potters – who passed it on to some Victorian china makers.

Originally the Nevers potters painted Persian or Chinese designs in opaque white on a blue enamel ground, which earned for the style the name of *bleu persan*. At Lambeth, some of the vases, jugs and mugs were also given these patterns, but others – and in my opinion much more happily – were covered with white splashes over the blue.

Niello

This is a form of DAMASCENING on silver. The lines cut in the design are filled with an alloy of silver, copper, lead, and powdered sulphur, which is fused and then polished. Some wonderful work in this way has been done all down the ages, especially in Italy of the fifteenth century, and later in Russia, especially the work of the well-known Tula factory.

Odd pieces of this sometimes turn up at sales: I recently saw a pretty little box in the shape of a pumpkin with stalk, leaves, and flowers, all worked with niello, sold for about three pounds. It may interest you to know that the first line engravings were paper proofs taken off early niello work.

Nightlights

Once upon a time, when we were very small and frightened of the dark, it was pleasant to have a light by one's bedside, soft enough to let our eyes droop, bright enough to let us have the comfort of falling asleep with our eyes on the familiar things in the room.

In the junk shops we will find plenty of these survivors of the days before bedside switches. There are those in blue and white Chinese porcelain, their light coming through grilles which throw marvellous patterns on the ceiling, moving and writhing in a draught. There are those in Staffordshire pottery in the shape of cottages and castles, which are getting dear now – and so being reproduced for us. There are stands in solid silver, complete with an extinguisher and glass shade: and by contrast there is one I have which is in tin, and looks like a miniature lighthouse.

'Nailsea' nightlight

Much sought after now are all those small affairs in different sorts of decorative glass. Prices of Battersea made one they dramatically called 'The Burglar's Horror': but other firms, like Palmers and Samuel Clarke, used a more tender kind of customer appeal by marketing brands with names like 'Glowworm', and 'Fairylite'. I have a tiny one bearing their name stamped on the base, and the shade is in 'Nailsea' stripes which gives a delightful effect. I have also seen larger ones, globular in shape, and in clear coloured glass, satin glass, Queen's Burmese glass, 'Bristol' blue, turquoise and green 'vaseline' glass. I have even seen, from the days before luminous dials, nightlight clocks with a little stand for the candle, and a leather case for taking it on a journey.

Nottingham Ware

Not very easily found nowadays are the fine brown stonewares, or BROWNWARE, with a rich sheeny salt-glaze, made at Nottingham in the eighteenth century.

Notable types were (1) jugs with double walls, the outer one being cut away with a pattern; (2) engraved 'decantors', i.e. jugs of a special shape, both

Nottingham carved jug

name and shape being used also in Jackfield Ware (*v. Looking in Junk Shops*); (3) mugs and wassail cups; and (4) best known of all, wares decorated with chips of clay like rough-cast on the side of a house. This was a distinctive feature of the Nottingham BEAR JUG.

Old Implements

If you take an old working implement away from its normal setting you will be struck with the interest and strangeness of its shape. When considered in this way a really old three-handled hayfork, a thin-tined muck fork, a long-bladed ditching spade, a wooden grain shovel, all take on an astonishing character not to be found in contemporary tools of the sort. So people are discovering that, in the right context, these things are electing themselves into material for decorating walls. I have seen country tea-serving barns and town espressos with walls left rough and crossed and broken up with the fascinating lines and arabesques of iron and wood provided by these old implements. Those who like to shove furniture around frequently will have their chance here: they can ring the changes to suit the mood of new purchases.

It need hardly be said that the place to find these things is the old farm building, the darkest corner of the blacksmith's shop, the derelict farm or cottage garden, the old mills and warehouses of country towns. Look, too, for those rotting wagons which in some parts of the country still lie where a Home Guard of twenty years ago put them in readiness to confound the Germans. There are lovely pieces of wood still unrotted, and fine shapes of ironwork.

18th-century iron grille

A penny-farthing bicycle is perhaps not an implement, but it hangs on a wall beautifully among all those straight lines. So do all those HALBERDS AND PARTISANS.

Old Scientific Instruments

By this I mean those relics of our scientific or mechanical past which have successively been superseded. The fact has been noted in the preceding paragraph that once a thing gets out-of-date its strangeness interests us, but it is also a fact that many pieces of early equipment, such as engines, carriages, mills, and the like, have an extraordinary beauty and simplicity of design. It is true that some of them, built in mid-Victorian times, are often embellished with the sort of ornament you might expect to find on temples rather than pieces of machinery. At the Great Exhibition of 1851 there was a cotton machine engine in the Ancient Egyptian style with a front rather like the Carreras building in London: another managed to find room among the wheels and pistons for some very tasty Gothic arches.

In the Science Museum, London, you will find a table lathe showing as many ROCOCO curlicues as

18th-century French dial compass

Mid-18th-century waywiser

the mirror on page 177. On the other hand, some spinning wheels are as tasteful expressions of, say, Hepplewhite, as you will expect to find. I find myself fascinated, too, with the lovely workmanship and delicacy of portable sundials and compasses in ivory and brass; of equinoctial ring dials, miniature globes, small orreries showing the movement of the earth, moon and planets, shagreen spyglasses, old telescopes and microscopes, beautifully chased mathematical and draughtsmen's instruments (in which field col-

Barometer

lectors look especially for the work of Michael Butterfield (1635–1724), who worked in Paris for much of his life. There are perpetual pocket calendars in silver and brass, bearing dates from the eighteenth century: hour-glasses in octagonal stands or cylindrical brass cases; astrolabes – forerunners of the sextant: zograscopes for viewing prints; 'Claude Lorraine' mirrors – which, if you want to paint a landscape like an old master, enables you to see your subject in tones rather than colours; magic lanterns and kaleidoscopes; the Camera Lucia for drawing objects in perspective or changing the scale of drawings; all sorts of weighing devices like miniature sets of scales and weights in fishskin cases; pinchbeck pedometers for measuring how far you have walked and dynamometers for showing the strength of your grip; all kinds of dipping, surveying and gauging instruments; and the delightfully named 'waywiser', perambulator or hodometer, a wheel with a diameter of thirty inches, with a dial attached, which you push along and measure distance in miles, furlongs, poles and yards.

Oriental Department

Fifty years ago every big department store had one of these, and in it, massed for inspection, you would

Sandalwood glove or handkerchief box

Syrian inlaid stool and tray stand

find those exotic things now sitting in lonely splendour among junk of other lands.

Elsewhere in this book will be found the better quality BIDRI WORK, the MORADABAD WARE. But here you have the Damascus brass jardinières for the aspidistra in the suburban window, in lacquered REPOUSSÉ work: they came in all sizes, from three inches in diameter to fourteen inches. There are also tray-stands from Cairo in carved and stained walnut, bearing large brass trays, probably from BENARES, though not the work that Anglo-Indians knew fifty years before. And there are those inlaid Syrian stools, with ivory, and decorated with little bobbins arranged in patterns: I have a magazine stand and a pot stand of this ware.

Japanese draught screens are, one supposes, a hangover from the JAPANESQUERY of the 1880s, but there they are with their gold embroidery on black or coloured grounds, or painted on light linen with landscape designs. For the dining-room, those with heavy embossed paper panels. Still in the Japanese corner, blue and white porcelain teapots with wicker handles, lacquer glove and hanky boxes, tea caddies, trinket boxes, and the rest. The junk paper sunshades, fans, handscreens and joss sticks could just as well have come from China, while the carved sandalwood boxes presumably came from India.

Palissy Ware

I have often wondered who buys these strange wall plaques crawling with lizards, crabs, insects, snakes and embellished with moss made from shredded clay. Finer dust-traps it would be difficult to conceive, but they go as regularly as they appear.

Apparently most of them came from Portugal early in this century, but similar wares were made by Frederick Thomas Mitchell at Rye in SUSSEX in the late nineteenth century.

Such things had a beginning in the work of Bernard Palissy, a French potter of the sixteenth century, so absorbed in his craft that he thought nothing of breaking up his furniture for fuel if he had a really important batch of pots in a firing.

Minton 'Palissy Ware' dish

There is another kind of Palissy Ware which has also been imitated here, especially at Mintons, using their famous 'majolica' glazes. These are usually large dishes and plaques with classical figures, ornamented rims in relief and in fine glazes of green, blue, yellow and red. If you want colour in pottery here it is: the type was a sensation when it appeared at the Great Exhibition in 1851.

Paste

This rather misleading word simply refers to a superior sort of glass used in JEWELLERY, and in case you think it is something invented by modern manufacturers, let me assure you that it was used not only by the Victorians, but by the Georgians, the medieval Italians, the Romans and the Ancient Egyptians: they valued it just as highly as the stone it imitated.

Many of our finds in the trays will be nineteenth- (and even eighteenth-) century imitations, made for the middle classes, of the splendid jewellery worn by the great ones.

Patina

This is a seductive word which will be offered you along with an old piece of furniture, bronze or pewter. 'Just *look* at that patina,' it will be urged, 'think how long it has taken to acquire *that*.'

Patina is truly a part of the delight one can take in things which were not made yesterday. Old oak, walnut, indeed most woods, acquire over ages of polishing and dusting and even mere existing, a special sort of colour texture which, even if the piece is a little faded or dried, it would be criminal to kill with a new French polishing.

Bronze picks up much of its subtle qualities of light and shade in brown or green, not only through the chemical action of the atmosphere but by years of gentle rubbing and cleaning. A gentle oxidisation was generally started immediately after casting by coating the piece with some special preparation: but only loving care, and the caress of silk, tweed or even the human hand will continue the good work. Serious bronze collectors treat their pieces like children.

Patina, like so many things, can be produced to order, and it is as well to look out for a coating of coloured wax. Other methods are not so easy to detect: there is, or used to be, a 'studio' in Paris where by judicious pickling, a thousand years could be added – and sometimes restored – to a piece in a fortnight. This would have been useful to the collector in the story (mentioned in *Nollekens*, I thought, but I cannot find it again) who, on being rather belatedly presented with a fine son, got into the habit, after the brandy bottle had been round several times, of having the nurse produce the baby to his dinner guests on a fine, antique bronze shield of enormous age and magnificent patina. But the nurse, who was just as proud of the child as his father, thought it a shameful thing to show her beautiful darling on such a dirty old thing, so one night, to the collector's horror, she appeared with the shield scoured as bright as a new brass candlestick.

His feelings must have been rather like mine when, only a few months ago, I fished under a table in a really junky shop and found a big heavy bronze bowl, beautifully worked in relief with a design of bears, and with a fine green patina. I asked the man how much he wanted. He said, 'I'll take a fiver for it as it stands, but if a dealer or collector don't have it soon

I'll polish it up bright and sell it to the public for two quid.' A baffling situation for me but an apt demonstration of the fact that patina can make up more than half the value of an old bronze.

Pearl Ware

The other day I found in a pile of plates a large heavy one with a bluish glaze. It had a Chinese pattern under the glaze, and at first I thought it was in fact Chinese porcelain: but on turning it over I saw it was marked 'pearl ware', together with an undecipherable and unidentifiable monogram.

This heavy earthenware, strengthened with flint and white clay, was originally developed by Josiah Wedgwood as an improved sort of creamware, and at first, since the intention was to imitate the pearly colour of nautilus shells, only enough cobalt was used to counteract the cream of the ware, resulting in a greeny tinge. But other Staffordshire potters, and also Leeds, used much more cobalt, with the very bluish result as shown in my plate.

Pearl ware was used not only for dinner services, but jugs, candlesticks and toilet sets: there were also figures on square bases in the same bluish glaze. Some of them were made by Neale. Spode's mark appears on pearl ware, and so does Davenport's.

Perambulators and Push Carts

If you want to give your larger infants something which they can satisfyingly feel no other children will have, look carefully around the junk sheds for old perambulators, go-carts and even tradesmen's push carts.

I know an antique shop window where can be seen a perambulator of about the 1840s, with a canopy

'Small Galloper' push chair

on top which makes it look so exactly like the 'surrey with the fringe on top' of *Oklahoma* that one wonders if that early American vehicle derived itself from an emigrating version. The dealer, of course, like another mentioned elsewhere, will not sell it because he finds it a wonderful attraction in his window. But neither will he clean it and paint it, which I find a very dog-in-the-manger attitude. Newly gilt, these Victorian baby carriages look enchantingly like the grown-up carriages of that day, just as a little earlier than that the children looked like miniature versions of an adult.

But perambulators are not the only quarry for the person who likes restoring things to their original glory of enamel and gilt. There is a place in London behind the stucco façade of a terrace, where in a stable a man is carefully renovating those little bakers' and other tradesmen's handcarts which used to be pushed around the streets. They make splendid toy caravans, which can be fitted up inside for dolls, or can even be turned into little sedan chairs. So don't only peer into junk sheds; look in the outhouses of friendly butchers and bakers and candlestickmakers.

If you want some guidance in your restoration work I would refer you to a little book I bought for three-pence the other day. Published about 1880, it is called *The Coach Painter's Hand Book and Guide*, by A Coach Painter of Thirty Years' Experience; and although the book is studded with references to a certain deceased manufacturer's paint and varnish (it seems to have been an early example of a 'sponsored' book), there is no doubt that the author knows his stuff, and won't let you skimp your job. Apart from priming, painting, rubbing, facing, varnishing, flatting and japanning, he discourses on the proper treatment of leather-covered carriages, basket carriages, and wicker work, writing, scrolling and ornamenting – and also gives you hints on how you would paint a locomotive engine if you owned one.

Photographic Pottery

I don't know if this is the official term to describe china and pottery decorated with photographic trans-fers, but the process has certainly been going long enough for such pieces to find their way into the junk shops.

One series often found is 'Royal Vistas' ware. There are milk jugs, very tall water jugs, vases, mugs, and other items in a white ware covered by a very distinctive yellowy-brown glaze, with gilding on the rim. The pictures are in black under this glaze, and although the mark claims that they are 'from Paint-ings by Various Artists', these are undoubtedly photographed rather than engraved: moreover, the paintings are accompanied by ordinary photographed views. The series bears the mark of Ridgways with their crown, but it must surely be after the firm was taken over in 1859 by Brown, Westhead

Moore, a firm which also had a great deal to do with colour printing in the Potlid (*v. Looking in Junk Shops*) field.

The reference books aren't much help with this sort of ware, so the interested collector will have to find his own way. As with the early ceramic lithography, it could be a very interesting one – and fabulously cheap to indulge in.

Piqué

Note well the accent over the 'e' in this word, for no sort of pique attaches to this entirely delightful method of decorating what the auctioneers usually call *objets d'art* – and we think of as pretty things we just want to have as many of as possible.

Piqué is a method of decorating tortoiseshell, mother-of-pearl, and ivory objects, such as trinket and snuff boxes, BONBONNIÈRES, etuis, trays, bouquet holders, can handles, etc., with gold and silver inlay. *Piqué point* is when the inlay is made up by means of little points of metal: *piqué clouté* uses larger points or 'nails' arranged in a pattern; while *piqué posé* is where the metal is laid on in flat cut-out shapes.

Late-18th-century piqué case

Either way, the work of the French and English craftsmen of the eighteenth century is quite exquisite and fetches high prices. But it is still possible to find Victorian specimens for very reasonable sums. It was fashionable in JEWELLERY, such as ear-rings, studs, pendants, necklets, brooches and bracelets, and there were also Card Cases (*v. Looking in Junk Shops*) with floral motifs in *posé* or *point*, sometimes both together; needle cases, writing sets, child's rattles, lorgnette cases, etc.

The early Victorian things tend to be heavier than those of the eighteenth century, though scarcely less skilful in the refinement of the work. By about the 'seventies mechanical means became available, and the decorations were stamped out and pressed into the tortoiseshell or mother-of-pearl between metal plates. All the same, some of these designs, on toilet articles such as brushes, hand-mirrors, trinket trays and the like are very pleasant and still adorn many a dressing table. It is, of course, *posé* or *clouté* work, the fine *point* decoration being a thing of earlier days. Watch out, however, for imitations in celluloid, with gold 'clous' simply stuck on: luckily these tend to flake off, thus giving the game away.

Although piqué lovers like to restrict the term to work on tortoiseshell, ivory, or mother-of-pearl, similar decoration is found on other materials like bone (for instance in LACE BOBBINS), SHAGREEN, HORN, woods of various kinds, even marble and agate.

Pig Jugs

Once upon a happy time it was the custom to drink the health of a bride and bridegroom out of a 'hogshead' of ale. This was made possible for ordinary mortals by using a 'hogshead' which was actually the

Sussex pig jug

cover of a jug made in the likeness of a pig. The same notion of a cup-cover is to be found in BEAR JUGS.

The only pig jugs – as distinct from Piggy Banks – I know are the ones made in SUSSEX. First, there is the traditional sort made in redware: its distinctive feature is that its ears and nose were long enough so that the cup would stand three-leggedly on the table. These are very rare now, dating probably from the early nineteenth century, so if you should find one in a cottage, do not be mean about it.

The second sort, considerably smaller in size, were made later in the century at Rye in SUSSEX RUSTIC WARE.

Pilgrim Bottle
This is a shape which has interested potters down the ages almost as much as the GOURD.

No need to question, one supposes, that it stems from leather bottles carried by pilgrims to shrines in the East, and that an early necessity was an arrangement whereby the thing could be slung over your shoulder, or from the belt: hence the two holes on either side of the mouth.

The earliest I have seen is one in a brown-glazed stoneware in the British Museum: it dates from T'ang days or earlier, i.e. well over a thousand years ago, The latest was made from slag, or what its makers.

Worcester pilgrim bottle (c. 1870)

Sowerbys of Newcastle upon Tyne, called 'vitro-porcelain': that blue ware made in the late nineteenth century which makes such a good price today. These flasks are usually impressed with a scene from a nursery tale.

In between these, the bottle turns up in early Ming blue and white – the Chinese called it the 'precious moon' vase, while Coalport, in the course of forging the wares and even the marks of Sèvres, Chelsea, Meissen and other factories, produced about 1850 some brilliantly coloured pilgrim bottles with imitation Japanese marks. Moore Bros of Longton made them in 'majolica' while Worcester used the shape in the course of its JAPANESQUEry.

All these, of course, merely use the form for its decorative quality; but in the early nineteenth century the SUSSEX potteries produced them in brown and cream glazed earthenware, not so much to go on pilgrimages to shrines, as to carry spirits home from the pub. Perhaps the most expensive sorts of pilgrim flask you can buy are those produced by Mintons in the last century in dark blue china, carrying the extraordinarily painstaking *pâte-sur-pâte* decoration evolved by Marc Louis Solon, whereby figures and whole groups were built up in relief by brush strokes of a slip paste.

Plaquettes

Here is a modest link between the junk shop and the collecting world of the great. Over the years I have come across, without particularly looking for them, small flat pieces of bronze, round, oval or square, with classical figures and scenes in relief. They seldom cost more than a few pounds, are often very beautifully modelled, and when you begin to put a few together you find that you have something like a miniature collection of bronzes. They look magnificent when set out in a bed of silk or velvet.

These small reliefs are not MEDALS, since they do not commemorate anything or any person, and are not plaques because they are scarcely big enough to hang upon a wall. They cover classical subjects like the Fall of Phaeton, Venus Chastening Cupid, Orpheus Descending into Hell, Hercules and the Nemean Lion, The Judgment of Paris, and so on: and biblical subjects such as The Judgment of Solomon, The Entombment, David and Goliath, The Adoration of the Magi. There are fine collections in the British, and Victoria and Albert, Museums; and only recently I saw a set of six German ones, with scenes from the New Testament, go for only eight pounds.

These plaquettes seem to have been made from the fourteenth to the sixteenth century, some as

Italian bronze plaquette

decorative panels on boxes, inkstands, candelabra, etc., which have come adrift from their original moorings. But there is also good reason for thinking that they were sometimes made as cheaper reproductions of pieces in gold and silver, and also of priceless intaglio gems. This seems to make them the equivalent of the print for the man who cannot afford an oil painting, or the Minton vase for the hard-up admirer of Sèvres. It seems, then, that there were junk-shop haunters with more taste than money even in Renaissance times.

Plate Pail

Often to be seen, but inexplicably high-priced, is the Georgian or early Victorian plate carrier, a pail-shaped affair with an opening on one side. When fretted or otherwise decorated it is a pretty enough thing, and I suppose you could hang it up and put a FLOWER POT in it.

But when solid or brassbound the only place for it is, probably, in an old-fashioned club.

Poker Work

Who has not sat in the saloon bars of pubs and gazed at those wooden plaques on which somebody with a hot poker has drawn archly worded mottoes or whimsical rhymes? I do not know if the industry still exists, but its handiwork does, and is likely to be with us for a long time yet.

But do not imagine that this is the best that can be done with a hot poker. If you look relentlessly in the junk shops you will find such articles as glove boxes, photograph frames, pipe-racks, blotter cases, playing-card boxes and other items decorated in this way with floral and other patterns. There are even, though not

Whitewood cabinet frames traced for pokerwork

very often, full-scale pictures with work emulating, and very much in the style of, wood engravings.

Dismiss from your mind also the idea that, having knocked up their box or whatever, the characters who made these things simply shoved a poker in the fire, pausing only to mull their lemonade with the orange-bright tip of iron, before drawing their patterns free-hand. On the contrary, they bought their virgin pieces, already traced out with a design from a shop: and so far from using a poker, they bought an outfit consisting of a platinum point heated by 'benzoline gas' from a little bottle. You could even pack the outfit away and take it on your seaside holiday.

Amateurs of old oak will note that small woodware of Stuart times was decorated with a hot poker or needle, sometimes very crudely, sometimes with vigorous peasant designs.

Portobello

Nobody can collect for very long without coming across this famous name. Denizens of, and visitors to, London will know the Portobello market, near Notting Hill, worth a visit any day (except closing day – Thursday) for its antique shops, and on Saturdays for its street stalls. The latter are full of everything, much

of it having been aired the previous day at the Cale-
donian Market (now in Bermondsey).

Portobello's speciality is silver and other metals,
and as with other street markets nowadays you must
no longer expect to find exquisite things unrecognised
and underpriced. But if you are collecting 'out of
step' with everyone else, here is the place for bargains.
If you want 'new' antiques you can find these also at
wholesale prices quite nearby.

We also meet the word Portobello on porcelain,
earthenware and china, especially on the famous
'Admiral Vernon' jugs. It may seem a strange coinci-
dence that a junk market should have set itself up in
a lane with a name used on old pottery, but in fact
both lane and pots have a common origin. They
commemorate the exploit of Admiral Vernon on 21st
November, 1739, in taking with only a handful of
ships the practically impregnable port of Portobello,
on the Chagré River in South America. It created a
sensation as a fine feat of naval daring, and the nation
proceeded to put the Admiral's portrait on everything,
including the Staffordshire jugs with the coloured
Pratt ware (v. *Looking in Junk Shops*) decoration and
PUNCH BOWLS.

And Portobello Lane? Another bit of social history
here, for about that time many farmhouses were being
rebuilt, not in the villages, but out in the newly
enclosed farmlands. Some of them were dubbed
Portobello, and there was one at the end of Portobello
Lane.

Hence also the Portobello Pottery near Edinburgh,
a famous source of earthenware figures ('dabbities')
and other items similar to Staffordshire wares. It is
interesting to note that Vernon's exploit was just in
time to get itself on to Delftware in its last days: a

19th-century Portobello Highlander

fine plate in the Victoria and Albert Museum bears a detailed map of the operation in Chagré River.

Portrait Miniatures

Not quite so fabulously expensive as is sometimes imagined are those rather charming little pocket-size portraits one sees grouped together on walls or in cabinets.

Portrait miniatures have always been extraordinarily popular in England and some very fine portraitists have devoted themselves to this branch of the art. Most people will have seen in countless reproductions the exquisite work of Nicholas Hilliard and his son Lawrence – they were the 'King's Limners': Holbein worked as a 'limner' too. The collectors also look for the work of celebrated artists like the Olivers, John Hoskins, Samuel Cooper, Richard Cosway, Andrew and Nathaniel Plimer, George Engleheart, and others.

But that 'others' covers a host of very able painters, and some charming examples of their work – portraits of girls, ladies, officers, beaux – can be picked up at no very great cost, many for less than twenty pounds, and quite a few for below ten.

In a recent sale I saw a nice Cosway of a lady, with a very elaborate powdered hair-do in tiers and a small cap on top of it, which made only eleven pounds, while a portrait of John Smart, one of the very finest of miniaturists, made only twenty. If you think that even these prices are high for such a little picture, reflect that just as much work could go into them as a large one. During the height of the craze for portrait miniatures most of them were painted in water colours on ivory using a delicate stippling or hatching technique. They were also done on paper and vellum. For this reason everyone who has a miniature ought to take very great care of it, not to let it get too dry or the ivory will warp, and certainly not to leave it in the full light of the sun, or like all water colour it will fade away. Museums, you may note, usually cover theirs with a curtain.

Portrait miniatures are still being painted, some, it is said, from not very creditable motives, so if you are asked high prices, look carefully at the asker. But they are also being painted still in a perfectly genuine way, and there is a Royal Society of Painters of Portraits in Miniature which holds regular shows: there is also at least one gallery in the West End of London where you can order a miniature of yourself or anyone else who happens to interest you. The last time I saw the price I think it was about £20.

Posset Pots

Like CAUDLE, posset was another of the strange drinks beloved of our ancestors. In it, cream or milk was associated with hot wine and much spicing or sweetening.

Early-18th-century posset pot

The early posset pots were round and lidded, with several handles – rather like a tyg – but posset was also, it appears, served in pots with spouts. They came in silver, pewter, delftware, slipware, glass and porcelain.

If you find such a pot and decide to make some posset in it this Christmas, you should observe the ancient custom whereby you drop into the steaming liquor a piece of silver and also your wife's wedding ring. You then invite a guest to fish around in it with a spoon. Whoever finds the ring is assured of a speedy marriage, whereas he or she who dredges up the coin keeps it as possibly more tangible evidence of good luck.

Powder Blue
This very delightful blue, which is variously mottled, granulated or white-specked, and which takes gilt decoration so felicitously, has been used on Chinese porcelain since Ming times, and also, by derivation, on Continental and English porcelains. Worcester were very keen on it, and used it with their reversed white panels of birds and flowers. The effect was achieved by preparing the piece with oil, then blowing powdered pigment on to the surface through a gauze-ended pipe.

19th-century powder flask

Powder Flasks

Often called powder horns because so many of them
were simply that – a horn mounted with silver or
some other metal – these have their interest for the
collectors of byegones, especially of firearms. Everyone who toted a blunderbuss, a flintlock fowling piece,
a musketoon or a highwayman's pistol, had to have
some means of carrying his powder and keeping it
dry: so there were flasks, large ones for the charge
powder, small ones for the flash powder. They come
in leather, wood, brass, copper, silver and gold.

Beautiful work has gone into the making of some
of these flasks, with inlay, embossing, engraving and
carving. Often they were made EN SUITE with the guns
or pistols, but you won't often find them together.
Earlier specimens are worked by hand, but in the
nineteenth century they tended to be stamped from
dies, often with shell patterns or elaborate hunting
scenes.

Don't expect to find them all actually horn-shaped.
There were flat round ones, like a PILGRIM BOTTLE;
dumpy affairs like a bag of sweets clutched in a small
hand; conical ones with a flat top, and others in

special shapes, such as a rifle butt. Dixons of Sheffield (famed for their BRITANNIA WARE) were prominent makers, and you sometimes find their name stamped on copper or leather flasks.

Sunderland lustre punchbowl

Punchbowls

A large bowl is a fine thing to set off a fine sideboard or cabinet. It is even finer when you can take the bowl down on high days and holidays and fill it with hot, steaming punch.

In the old days no family who liked their friends to come and see them failed to have the means of putting up a brew of punch. The name of this cheerful beverage is said to derive from the Hindustani word *panch* or the Persian *punj*, meaning five, after the five qualities necessary to a good punch: that it should be hot, cold, bitter, sweet and strong. To provide these qualities the anglo-Indian nabobs who brought

us the drink used sugar, lime juice, water, spice and a
villainous concoction called arrack. In England, rum
and brandy were preferred.

Punchbowls, according to their period, came in
various sorts of pottery – delftware, stoneware, porcelain, creamware, bone china, ironstone china and
its variations. I once had one, together with its perforated colander, in ordinary BROWNWARE, which
shows that even the humble home liked its bowl of
grog. Decoration was a great feature of these bowls,
of course, and they range from heraldic and Chinese
designs to ships, political slogans, and the rest, all in
the familiar processes of transfer printing, painting,
lustreing and so on. There are very competent reproductions of these about, and also some fine modern
versions issued as commemoration bowls.

You can find lordly ones in silver and Sheffield
Plate, with spreading feet: but, surprisingly, few glass
ones.

Queen Anne

We probably overwork this word as an indication of a
period of style, for the good lady reigned only from
1702 to 1714.

What we all probably mean by it is the moment
when the English cabinet makers and architects began
seriously to tame the flowing lines of the Netherlands-
BAROQUE and evolved a distinctive English style. It
was an age of quiet restraint, comfort, elegance. The
cabriole LEG became established, mainly with a club
or pad foot, also the scallop shell and the acanthus leaf.
People delighted in delicately made cabinets and small
tea tables for their Chinese porcelain and exquisitely
made little BONHEURS DU JOUR.

They liked marquetry, lacquer and also two-person

Queen Anne secretaire-cabinet

settees which they preferred to call love-seats (see SETTEES). Delftware was still about, also some of our loveliest silver.

Regency
Strictly speaking the Regency of George, Prince of Wales, lasted only from 1811 to 1820, but the term goes for the whole period – say 1790 to 1837 (thus leaving out poor old King Billy), in which the austerities of the ADAM style, *derived* from classical

Regency console table

models, began to be replaced by actual copies of them, also of exotic forms like the Egyptian.

In France it became 'Empire', hence the expression, 'English Empire'. All the same, things in good late Georgian taste continued to be made, especially in the provinces.

Repoussé Work

Perhaps the most frequently met with sort of decoration of metals, meaning literally 'pushed back'. It is done by putting your metal object upon a bed of pitch or wax (or if it is hollow, filling it with same), and then hammering out a design with blunt punches of various shapes and sizes. EMBOSSING is repoussé work done from the back of the piece: CHASING from the front of it, and much lovely work is produced by a combination of these. *Chasing*, as a term, is also used to describe the finishing touches given to cast work; but if you cut lines in the metal you are *engraving* it.

Rice Grain Porcelain

Still coming into the country from somewhere in the Orient, presumably Hong Kong, are modern versions of the well beloved rice grain china, of which one often sees sets in the shops.

Some people are curious to know how this effect is brought off. The little translucent holes in the shape of rice grains are cut in the side of the vessel before the glaze is applied, and it is this which fills in the holes. You are therefore looking through a kind of little window made of glass.

For once the Chinese seem not to have originated this idea, but to have lifted it from the Persians in what was called their 'Gombroon' work. Rice grains indicate abundance in Chinese symbolism, so perhaps we should have included this under CHARMS.

Rings

Every jewel box has its quota of rings, so does every secondhand jewellery shop. And every ring has its little story – who bought it, how long ago, where and why.

Some of the rings you see are so large or 'old-fashioned' looking that it seems unlikely they will ever get worn again. But why not mount them in a case, as the jewellers do, and as they do with the magnificent collection in the Victoria and Albert?

What sort of rings are there – apart, I mean, from the materials of which they are made? Signet rings have been looked at under SEALS, but there are all the engagement or betrothal rings: once upon a time there was no distinction between the two. There are token rings too, such as the 'Gimmal', with its part-able parts which come together to show clasped hands; there is the 'Regard' ring with seven hoops and a stone on each which spells out the word with the initial letters of the stone; there are the lovers' knots, the Mizpah ('I will watch over thee') ring; there are rings with guards; snake rings; wishbone rings.

Chinese rings often bear characters conveying a message if you can find somebody to read it – maybe wishing you 'riches and public honours' or 'long life

15th-century silver betrothal rings

17th-century gold puzzle ring with three hoops and
Gimmal betrothal or wedding ring

and riches'. There are very precious rings with tiny
watches in them; there are smokers' rings with a
tobacco tamper mounted; there are swivel rings with
two sides to show. 'Surprise' rings open up and show
some magic sign; memorial rings are among the
MEMENTO MORI with the locks of hair, inscriptions or
death's head; there are puzzle or magic rings, with
all their baffling hoops. Fraternity rings like those in
Freemasonry bear the symbols of the societies.

I suspect that these unusual, and today rather un-
wearable, rings, where there is good material and
workmanship, will greatly appreciate in value before
very long.

Rococo
Rococo in the junk shop will probably be Revived
Rococo, which is a VICTORIAN STYLE. But, for the
record, for that chance find of a Gesso wall bracket
or mirror frame, and otherwise for your visits to the
museums, this word signifies that style which suc-
ceeded BAROQUE and characterised the reign of
LOUIS XV. Here are those wild 'C' curves, asymmetrical
(or 'skew-whiff') designs, seen here much in the form
of ormolu clocks and the aforesaid wall-brackets,
bulging commodes, and a general effort to treat wood
as though it were melted down and poured into
moulds.

Mid-18th-century rococo gilt mirror

The style swept through Europe, representing feminine to BAROQUE's masculine, often mixed itself up with Chinese and GOTHIC, left a mark on English porcelain, especially at Chelsea; and was finally overpowered by ADAM.

Rummer

Shall we try to settle the old argument about the rummer? Most people assume that this means what it implies; that it is a glass for the drinker of rum. If you point out that although the stem is much shorter than that of a goblet, the bowl is quite as big, and would hold enough rum to make even a three-badge A.B. blink sharply, then they reply that it wasn't intended for neat rum but for grog, i.e. rum, hot water and spice.

The scholars, on the other hand, claim that the word derives from the Dutch *roemer*, signifying 'Roman style', or alternatively from a lady named Anna Roemers Visscher (1583–1651), who decorated a lot

19th-century rummer with cup-shaped bowl and late
17th-century roemer

of such glasses with flowers and fruit. These *roemers*,
by the way, are very like the hock glasses you found
still in use when last you worked your way through
the winegardens of the Rhineland.

But another, and more thoughtful, school has noted
that the Lower Rhenish word *roemer* means 'to boast';
also that when they arrived in England they did so
at the same time as Rhenish wine. So the most tenable
view, I think, is that they came over here as *roemers*, or
'boasters', got shorter in the stem and were found
handy for grog; then became anglicised as rummers.
The boasting, no doubt, was anglicised as well.

Sang de Boeuf
You will see Chinese bottles and vases covered with a
deep and very beautiful mottled blood-red glaze,
which, like the ox-blood after which it is named, coagu-
lates here and there into deep sherry-brown. It first
appeared as one of the copper glazes developed in
China in the reign of K'ang Hsi (1662–1722), and
was revived with great success in the late nineteenth

century on English pottery by Bernard MOORE, William MOORCROFT, BURMANTOFTS and others. See also FLAMBÉ.

Satsuma Ware

That type of pottery which now goes under this name – a creamy buff ware smothered with gilding and painting and brocading – is at the moment 'out'. You will find it in all the shops; it comes as bottles, large and small vases, boxes and other items, and in spite of the disapproval of the cognoscenti it somehow goes – I suspect to the Italians, who buy everything, or to the Americans, who buy anything.

What troubles the serious collectors is that they happen to know of a fine eighteenth-century ware from Satsuma Province in Japan, covered with a cream or ivory crackled glaze, with most restrained enamelled and gilt decoration in the true Japanese taste. The wares sent to us in the last century, however, were a rather insulting parody of this, especially made for nineteenth-century Europeans, whose love for having every square inch of everything covered with decoration was well known to the wily Japanese merchants cashing in on the JAPANESQUE craze of the 'seventies and 'eighties. Under that head are discussed the Worcester imitations of Satsuma.

So here is a ware which the Japanese have gone to a great deal of trouble about, and we don't want to buy it. One day, perhaps, when there is no Japanese handcraft left, we may.

Scale Blue

Almost a trade mark of early Worcester are the fish-scale grounds, mostly in blue, surrounding the reserved panels in which were painted all the exotic birds and flowers so much beloved of collectors. Wares with these panels left blank were often sent out to outside decorators for painting. These scales, and other methods of breaking up the blue ground, such as diapers and tiny circles like SHAGREEN, seem to have been a Worcester invention.

Seals

There was a time when all of us who had any business with documents, or wrote letters to any extent, carried a seal – or had one on our writing tables and desks.

Many of these seals are still about, for some of them are really pieces of JEWELLERY, and not to be lightly thrown away, even if their function has passed away. So today in the shops you can find them set into RINGS – when of course they become signet rings, made of gemstones like carnelian, onyx, emerald and bloodstones, carved at first with crests, later with any sort of device which would please a buyer.

More collectable than these, because of the fine work that went into their handles, are the desk seals. Wedgwood moved in on this fashion by making them with handles of lilac or blue jasper ware; they also appeared in the delightful Chelsea porcelain 'toys' and Bilston enamels. Jade, rock crystal, ivory, smoked quartz, coloured glass, jet, onyx, were all called into use, beautifully worked and sometimes modelled into animals' heads and other shapes.

Those who like using seals for their letters may be interested in some tips given by the late Dr George Williamson, who insisted that everyone, especially ladies who had important and perhaps confidential letters to write, ought to re-learn the art of sealing. What he recommends is, don't just shove the wax

into the flame and blob a shapeless mass on the paper:
it looks horrible. Your graceful sealer revolves the
wax carefully above the flame until it is soft, then
rubs it gently on the envelope in an ever-decreasing
circle until there is a nice shape. She then gets some
Chinese vermilion of the very finest quality, rubs a
tiny portion over the seal with a camel's hair brush,
warms the seal by breathing on it so as to prevent
adhesion to the wax, then applies it very, very gently
and firmly. She blows off the loose vermilion from
the border, and has her impression in rich vermilion
beautifully framed in sealing wax red. And off it
goes, by hand messenger, to some lucky man.

Secret Compartments

How easy dealers find it to break down our sale re-
sistance when a piece of furniture has a secret drawer
or compartment in which we can put our most private
papers, or mystify a guest with its ingenuity. More
attractive still is the thought that you may find
another drawer, of which the dealer is unaware, probably still containing some priceless relic.

Simplest of these tricks is the panel which to our
surprise opens and reveals a nest of drawers: more
subtle is that in which a nest of open pigeon holes
pulls forward and discloses a cupboard or shallow
drawer where we thought there was only the back
of the desk. Sometimes a drawer pushes *back* instead
of forward, releasing a catch which opens a recess
when you pull the drawer out again.

If you suspect secret compartments in a piece the
first and most obvious thing to do is to take outside
measurements, then the inside measurements of the
various spaces inside, making allowances for the
thickness of the wood. If your calculations leave any

spaces unaccounted for, then you set to work very gently pressing this and pulling that, bearing in mind that these things always work on some principle of sliding, swivelling, locking and springing by counter-weights, or some other means.

How about going to work on that little Davenport left you by Aunt Jemima? Could *that* have been where she left all her money?

Serpentine
When a COMMODE or a desk, or some other piece of furniture, has a front which undulates in a snaky line, it is said to be Serpentine; when this is combined with a bulge the other way, as in BOMBÉ, you probably have something very BAROQUE, or ROCOCO.

Services
I have sometimes wondered to see people paying largish sums for odd Coalport or Copeland plates, cups and saucers because they like them, and then buying one of the less attractive sort of new tea or dinner services because, presumably, they think they couldn't possibly afford a whole service of old things they like.

They ought some day to go along to one of the larger sales in the big towns, and see what modest prices are sometimes fetched by the old services. Last year, for example, I saw a Davenport tea and coffee service painted in puce *camaieu* with sprigs of flowers and fluted rims, forty-four pieces in all, sold for only ten pounds. I realise that not everyone wants over forty pieces, but at that price you could afford to give away part sets even if you don't want to sell them to a dealer to dispose of piecemeal.

But if you do want something smaller, but more

Nankin ware dinner service

exciting, how about a Rockingham claret ground ten-piece dessert set, each piece painted with a different botanical sketch of a flower – they included narcissus, pansies, tulips, nasturtiums, and roses? This made twenty-eight pounds – much cheaper than you would buy those plates and dishes separately. Others I have seen included an attractive Chelsea Derby tea-set with an apple-green ground and painted in the Chinese taste with flowering plants and roots, with scattered sprigs and insects, twenty-nine pieces for thirty-five pounds; there also was a Flight Worcester tea-set which sold for ten shillings a piece; a Coalport one painted with baskets of flowers for the same; another big and superbly painted Rockingham tea and coffee service with fully blown roses for about fifteen shillings a piece; a huge Mason's Ironstone dinner set in a red, blue and yellow Japan pattern, fifty-six pieces at ten shillings each; and an early Copeland and Garrett tea and coffee service with panels and flowers on a green and gilded ground, twenty-eight pieces for twenty-two pounds.

All these services, of course, include their teapots, jugs, basins, or tureens, dishes, etc., as the case may be, so you can see how comparatively cheaply it works out. It is also worth comparing these prices with what it would cost you to buy new sets.

Settees, Sofas, and so on

Some people like to sit on their own, in which case they use (in the West) CHAIRS; others like to stretch out full length with their feet up; a few others like to sit down close to their fellow creatures. For all these the junk shops offer a variety of fare, and it may be useful if we try to sort out some terms, like settee, settle, *chaise-longue*, day-bed, couch, love-seat, Chesterfield, davenport, ottoman, divan, and the rest.

I suppose we should start historically with a *settle*, which is an advance on a plain form or bench in that it has arms as well, or ends as well as a back; this back can be low (like our Cromwellian one) or high (like the one from a country pub). There are also settles in the *Windsor, Ladder-back and Spindle-back* families described under CHAIRS.

In the process of becoming a *settee* the settle seems to have acquired an upholstered seat and arms, and this led to the more luxurious *Sofa*, an eighteenth-century term from the Arabian *soffah*. But, on the way there, the settee could not help reminding itself that as well as being a settle, it could also be two, or even

Oak settle

19th-century oak cottage or inn settle

three, chairs. This is clearly to be seen in our QUEEN ANNE two-chair-backed settee with its interestingly simple Cabriole leg.

A *couch* could be like a *sofa*, as shown in our early Victorian one, but I have always felt that it was really closer to the *day-bed*, in that you ought to be able to lay full length on it – a close relation of the article of furniture which a famous actress referred to when she remarked how pleasant it was to exchange the hurly-burly of the *chaise-longue* for the peace and quiet of the marriage bed. In both of these your head rested on a pillow, kept in place by a head board; whereas with a sofa or couch you could recline against the sloping end.

The *Ottoman*, another full-length job, was really an upholstered box, often with a head at one end which let down; the *divan*, simply an upholstered seat with neither back nor sides which in female bachelor rooms became a *divan bed* – all rather confusing because the terms have themselves changed in their use. We could with reason say that our *window-seat*, and *love-seat*, also the pleasant *Knole* affair with its loose cushions and bobbin hangings, are all *settees*, whereas the *couch* and the *day-beds* are not. So too, is the 'Walton, richly inlaid and covered with Genoa velvet', which

Queen Anne two-chair-backed settee

we were buying from Harrods at the end of the century.

A newcomer from late Victorian days is the *Chesterfield*, a big upholstered settee generally with its matching pair of armchairs: presumably that is what the Americans call a *Davenport*, a name reserved in Britain for that pleasant little writing desk which has drawers opening to the side.

Well, couch, settee, sofa, they are all there, awaiting the imaginative eye. Compared with the cost of new,

Queen Anne love seat

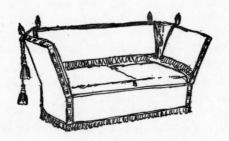

18th-century window-seat (*top*); Knole settee (*middle*);
17th-century day-bed (*bottom*)

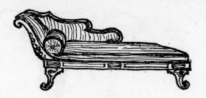

Early-Victorian couch

even with fresh upholstery and covering, they are not dear. Personally I would look very hard at those from the Edwardian era. Craftsmanship just then was excellent, better even than in late Victorian days, and there was an elegance which almost foreshadowed that of 'modern'.

S'Graffiato

One of the simplest ways of decorating any kind of pot or bowl is to cover it with a glaze and, while this is still wet, cut or scrape through it so that you reveal the colour of the body beneath, and so make a pattern. The word, I understand, is bad Italian for scratching.

In spite of its simplicity, s'graffiato in the right hands has always been a most effective means of decorating wares of the sort which attract us for their rough primitive textures. We are only now beginning to catch up with the fact that the early potters of China, Korea, and Persia, though they may have lived in mud huts, could get as much power and sensitivity into a scratched line as anyone in Chelsea today. Go and look at it in the museums: the modern studio potters have been entranced with it for years now, and the Wise Ones are quietly buying their work before somebody realises that, once again in ceramic history, there is an English way of being Chinese.

For a gallant and very pleasant and also very Doulton version of s'graffiato see the pots bearing the incised outline animals of Hannah Barlow (*v. Looking in Junk Shops*).

Shagreen

The word has a nice old-fashioned ring, and the articles decorated with it an equally nice old-fashioned look. There are small portable writing sets of the eighteenth century, etuis for the lady's handbag, penholders, knife and fork cases (for taking on your travels abroad by coach) swordhilts, spectacle cases, in fact, all objects likely to have a lot of wear, but at the same time needing to be pleasant to look at and handle.

Although most shagreen is dyed green, it comes in other colours as well, even white and grey. The word, in fact, has nothing to do with 'green' but derives from the French *peau de chagrin*, or ass's skin, which itself also gives rise to the other meaning of chagrin, i.e. mortification – presumably from one's having to ride on the rough skin of an ass. But this was only one source: it is also prepared from the skin of sharks, rays, and spotted dogfish. Nowadays, of course, you find imitations of it in hides patterned by copper plates and embossed paper.

Shaving Stand

Not many pieces of furniture in the last few centuries have been designed especially for men, so one welcomes the odd shaving stand one sometimes sees.

I bought one for myself only recently in a back street junk-shed for 'twopunten'; and I am already very fond of it. The mirror is small and octagonal, but adjustable to the unshaven chin, and you can

bare your teeth into it comfortably. The top of the
stand is prettily galleried with bobbin turning, there
is a cupboard big enough to carry all necessary gear
and tackle, and the rails at the sides carry hucka-
back towels. Somebody has obligingly removed the
old French polish, and in its naked mahogany it
looks well with the ladder back and cane chairs in
my bedroom.

Perhaps the most desirable feature of these items is
that they are hopelessly inadequate as dressing tables
for women; consequently one can not only buy them
cheaply, but keep them for one's own use.

Ships in Bottles

How does the ship, masts stepped and sails trimmed
for a fair wind, get through the narrow neck of the
bottle? The answer is that it doesn't – at least not in
sea-going order. First the sea itself is made up of
cork, putty, sand and glue, painted realistically, poked
in with a wire or needle, and glued in place. Then the
hull is carved and masts and spars are cut and rigged,
but packed flat for insertion through the neck, leaving
thread lines for pulling up. The ship is stuck in posi-
tion, the maker hauls away handsomely on the thread
lines and drops a spot or two of glue here and there
to make all secure.

These models were made all through the nineteenth
century, and are priced according to the workmanship, and, sometimes, when they commemorate a
particular ship. If you want to find your way among
the named ones, there are plenty of reference books
and histories. I have not seen any steamers, except
for some very early hybrids; but most of the men who
like doing these things were either brought up in sail
or like to think they were.

Has anyone yet seen an aeroplane or a space-ship in a bottle?

Shop Signs

Many are the covetous eyes which are lifted to the large old signs which still hang over tradesmen's or craftsmen's premises, or perhaps stand in their windows. Everyone over the age of fifty will remember when the kilted Highlander (or was he a Lowlander?) was as common in the doorway of a tobacconist as an Indian in an American cigar store: he advertised, I believe, Scottish snuff – then considered the best. An ironmonger's shop might hang out a huge pad-lock, presumably made of painted wood, and a sports outfitter's a tennis racket of dimensions which would add considerably, I am sure, to the interest of games on the Centre Court at Wimbledon. The huge col-oured and gilded pots of the colourmen, the bottles with tinted glass in chemists' windows, the outsize hand and boot of the glovemaker and bootmaker respectively; the black and gilt canister of the grocer (or Italian warehouseman, as I think he is still called in some places), are still to be seen, together with all

Hardware shop sign

the figures outside inns, such as Red Cows, Bears with Ragged Staffs, Swans, White Harts, Red Lions, and the rest.

These items, as soon as they become prised away from their moorings through demolition, appear in the shops along with the ships' figureheads, and as they soon disappear they must be eagerly wanted. There is one item so popular, in fact, that it is being made again: this is the large pig's head which once appeared in the windows of pork butchers. I know where you can buy half a dozen of these new, all in nice tissue paper.

Silver Mounts

Silver is expensive nowadays, so why not look at those things in which the metal is used sparingly? In another place I have mentioned COCONUT CUPS, and after all, PIQUÉ (though far from cheap) is a sort of silver mounting. There are silver-mounted photographs from Edwardian sitting-rooms which have fine work in them; there are leather glove boxes and blotters, travelling watch cases, perpetual calendars; cigar and spectacle cases, toilet things like hairbrushes, mirrors, combs and the rest; and there are all manner of little wooden things.

But it is probably in the field of glass that one finds the most attractive things. Old mounted cut-glass only doubles one's difficulties by putting together two equally expensive materials; however, there are many nice late Victorian or Edwardian items like silver-mounted claret jugs and decanters, salad bowls, spirit and scent bottles, glass pepper mills, cruets, inkstands, etc.

It would be interesting to see a shelf of really well

selected late silver-mounted glass, and it would hardly cost a fortune to put together.

Snuff Bottles

Peer into the table show cases of some shops and you will see a lot of little bottles, not only of glass, but of porcelain, ivory, various kinds of gemstones and other materials. Some of them are quite plain, others are beautifully carved and worked in Chinese styles, which really are Chinese styles and not designs specially made for export to us foreign devils.

A few years ago you could have brought together a collection of these bottles for very little money, but in case you think that I am merely tantalising you with nostalgic stories of the past, let me add that I don't consider them dear even at today's prices. With miniature works of art like these little bottles one has to bear in mind three things. One is that the value of our money is decreasing anyway: another that this sort of craftsmanship – which entails perhaps months of work for very little money – is dying out: the third, that there are more people about today with money to buy such articles. So when you find that you are asked anything from two to twenty-five pounds for them remember that you are buying unique small works of art which will probably never be made again.

As to the materials of these bottles, at the top end of the price range you will find them hollowed out of the solid jade so beloved of the Chinese, and therefore given the most exquisite carving and finishing. Amethyst bottles are also dear, like those in other hardstones such as lapis lazuli, turquoise, alabaster and the rest. In glass, some are imitations of hard-

Chinese glass snuff bottle with bat symbol for longevity

stones, with much overlay work whereby various kinds of different coloured glass were cut through to show the coloured layers (like our CAMEO GLASS). There are also many which are painted *inside* the glass bottle in enamels. Porcelain bottles repeat all the lovely effects of coloured glazes such as FLAMBÉ or SANG DE BOEUF: and there are modest little affairs in the familiar and less costly 'blue and white'. Other materials are cloisonné and painted enamel, lacquer, bronze, tortoiseshell, mother-of-pearl, silver, coral and amber. Shapes vary enormously, from small cylinders to flat flasks, or even fruit, animals, humans. The GOURD is a great favourite.

One sometimes sees small lots of snuff bottles appear in the sale rooms, and this offers an opportunity for the collector who likes to save his money for a splash. Only last season I saw a little bunch of twenty-three bottles, including two in porcelain moulded with the Eighteen Lohan, and three in green glass and another in the form of double GOURDS, go for thirty-two pounds, i.e., about thirty shillings each: while another lot of thirteen – including six porcelain ones attractively moulded with figures, one in carved amethystine quartz, a glass one overlaid on a turquoise ground – made about three pounds apiece.

Ideally your snuff bottles, if they are Chinese and not made in Europe, should have a stopper with a small spoon attached to it. This was necessary to the Chinese gentleman because of his long carefully kept fingernails. It seems to me a highly civilised way of taking snuff.

Soapstone

Most of the carvings one sees in this browny-grey-green mottled stone are rather unappetising flower holders made in the form of rocks and trees and with a curiously flattened appearance. These abound in the shops and nobody seems to want them. But there are also more ambitious carvings of animals, of the EIGHT IMMORTALS and Shou Lao, of 'Immortal maidens' and of figures kneeling before shrines. I have also seen book-ends, lacquered in red and carved with DOGS OF FO, and a figure of the latter playing with eight puppies, five of them climbing on his back (it was the father, the one with the ball). There are also SNUFFBOTTLES in soapstone – which, it may be of interest to note, is actually steatite or talc, the softest of the gemstones on the Mohs scale (see JEWELLERY).

Spinning Wheels

Pleasant to have an old 'cottage' type spinning wheel if you have an old cottage. Well, they are not all that difficult to find if you watch the sales carefully, and also look out for the modern reproductions which wouldn't spin a yarn to convince anyone.

But the spinning wheel has a long history, and if you are really interested you will find it worth while learning a little about spinning. Originally the wool was spun in the fingers, using a weighted stick to set the yarn twisting and winding into a thread: all you had was a distaff carrying the yarn, and a spindle or

'Castle' spinning wheel

weighted stick with which you wound it, thus producing the required combination of twisting and winding. The spinning wheel as we know it today seems to have been the invention of a German woodcarver named Johann Jurgens, working in the fifteenth century, but it seems more likely that he improved the mediaeval pattern, which either wound or twisted, but didn't do both at once.

Those made for cottages or farm houses were from hard woods like yew, box and oak, but without much trimming, except for the usual turning. These do not cost a great deal even now: I saw two go for fourteen pounds in a sale recently. But there is another race which will cost you a good deal more for it was intended for the drawing-room, and so had to look as handsome as the rest of the things there. These are of walnut, oak or ebony, sometimes inlaid with ivory or mother-of-pearl, in fact, quite beautiful small pieces of furniture.

Straw Marquetry
Just occasionally one comes across an example of a kind of marquetry in which straw was used for decoration instead of wood. There are work-boxes, tea-caddies, patch boxes, needle holders,

fire-screens, watchstands, picture frames and other items.

Although some work of this kind was done in the straw plaiting areas around Luton, most of it was turned out by French prisoners during the Napoleonic wars. Six thousand of them were housed in a great prison near Peterborough, and the museum there has a fine collection of the ware. Apparently the men went in for this particular use of straw because they were not allowed to compete with the local straw plaiting industry.

Pieces of straw were dyed in various colours then split with a special tool, some examples of which survive. The pieces were glued on to a 'carcase', often supplied by the customer. There is a fine example of a straw marquetry picture, a stylised landscape, in the Victoria and Albert Museum. Quite large pictures of buildings and views were also made on the Continent, especially in Austria.

Strike-a-lights

That race of people who can coax life out of the most obdurate small piece of mechanism will delight in finding members of the varied clan of tinder boxes, strike-a-lights, fire steels, and the rest.

A tinder box is essentially a receptacle for holding a piece of flint, a steel striker, and tinder, i.e., a substance which will easily ignite, such as charred rag. When, by dropping the spark expertly on to the tinder you get it to smoulder, you then have the problem of conveying this newly-created fire to whatever it was you wanted to set alight. This job is made easier if you have a sulphur match, which bursts into flame, lets off a most obnoxious smell, but lights your candle or fire. When one thinks what it must have been like

Early-19th-century pistol 'strike-a-light'

to try to light a candle in the middle of a wet steamy night one cannot fail to be impressed by the fortitude of our ancestors.

Some tinder boxes are of wood, with a sliding lid, often very finely carved, especially in the case of the Dutch ones. Another type is a circular tin box with an inner compartment for the tinder, and a candle holder on the outside of the lid, so that the box then performs the office of a candlestick. These boxes come not only in tin but also in brass, copper, and Sheffield Plate. As all nations were in the same boat as ourselves, so they all have their different sorts of boxes – or leather pouches or purses.

A more sophisticated means of making fire is the tinder pistol, or strike-a-light. This was obviously a development of the flintlock pistol, with tinder in a receptacle below the striker instead of gunpowder. This often had a little box at the side for the sulphur match and a candle holder as well. Some of the foreign

18th-century brass tinder box

sorts are beautifully engraved or inlaid: others are simple brass or steel frames with a wooden stock. On English ones, makers' names appear: I have noted Richards of London, among others.

I daresay you would have to pay ten pounds for a good specimen: but ones with parts missing are found more cheaply.

Stumpwork

Once upon a time pictures in stumpwork, either framed or on jewel or toilet boxes, fetched much higher prices than they seem to now – although they still cannot be regarded as cheap.

They are the forerunners, also made at home in the boudoir, of the eighteenth-century embroidered pictures, and they get their name from the 'stump' of hair or wool used to fill out the figures in the 'raised' needlework. They are often decorated with seed pearls, silver and gilt thread, lace and sequins.

Most of the subjects show biblical scenes, or perhaps the Stuart kings and queens, with a date; and the work has an artless simplicity which charms some people.

Early-17th-century stumpwork picture

Sunderland Bridge

Here is a subject which will keep you busy looking for a long time. Until I read the booklet on the Sunderland potteries (see READING LIST) I had no idea that the views of this famous bridge seen on the pottery, mainly lustre ware, were not all identical. But it seems there are many variations, which can be helpful in dating a piece.

First it should be pointed out that the structure's proper name is the WEARMOUTH BRIDGE, which at its opening in 1796 was the longest single-span cast-iron bridge in the world, with a span length of 236 feet and a height from low-water mark of 100 feet. Public interest in it was stimulated not only as a feat of engineering, but by the fact that following a bank failure the shares were distributed by lottery to 6,000 subscribers. The bridge was rebuilt in 1859 by Robert Stephenson, son of George Stephenson, and this 'new' bridge also appears on pottery.

The Sunderland Museum has pieces of pottery with twenty-eight different views of the WEARMOUTH BRIDGE, differing in the number of lamp-posts on it, shipping in the river, figures on the banks, whether the bridge is seen taken from the east, south-east, or west, before or after the new bridge was built.

Many of these pieces bear the marks, impressed or painted, of potters like Moore & Co., Hylton Pottery,

Sunderland Bridge view

Dawson & Co., Dixon & Co., Scott Southwick, etc., but most of those seen nowadays are unmarked, and present an exciting challenge to the intelligent collector.

Sussex slipware churn

Sussex Pottery

Sussex clay has been turned into pots for a very long time now, and occasionally a farm sale brings to light one of the old pitchers or harvest jugs, platters or bowls, with brown or yellow glaze and little or no decoration. So rare as to be museum pieces are the pilgrim flasks, tobacco jars, mugs and miniature churns with decoration of stars, or printers' types inlaid in a lighter coloured slip. The once famous Brede hedgehogs with indentations for quills are now almost a legend.

Fine earthenware pitchers with yellow and green glazes have been made in quite recent times and are still to be found, and while some of the traditional wares were made at Rye, another sort of pottery from there is sufficiently distinctive to earn it an entry under its trade name of

Sussex Rustic Ware

the special feature of which was applied decoration in the form of wreaths of hops. This was carried a

stage further by Frederick Thomas Mitchell (1864–
1920) whose work shows much more detail, the hops
and other forms standing out in such high relief that
it is not easy to find undamaged specimens. He also
produced a type of PALISSY WARE, and a latter-day
version of the Sussex PIG JUG. His aunt, widow of the
first Thomas Mitchell, produced among varied items,
a 'folding' jug with a twist in the body. The Rye
pottery is still going strong, but today it produces
quite different wares: the LOVING CUP is a pleasant
example.

Tables
As with chairs, so with tables: there are so many one
hardly knows where to start.

Our pictures show one or two interesting ones.
There is the rosewood *Sofa* table, for use, as its name
suggests, by the side of the sofa. It has shallow drawers
and usually flap ends for lengthening in case somebody comes to tea. They started in the eighteenth
century, and the Sheraton ones often sported that
designer's favourite lyre-ends with sabre feet. Good
ones have become enormously more expensive than

Regency sofa table

Chippendale console table

most small tables, probably because with the smaller households of today they have been found to make convenient and elegant dining tables. In a way it is a longer version of the *Pembroke*.

The *Console* (really an architectural term for a bracket; it was originally called a 'clap') is a table which has only two legs (or even one) and is fixed to a wall, usually under a mirror which will reflect the gorgeous ornaments borne upon it: but the word is also used of any narrow table which stands against a wall. Our specimen is a gilt Chippendale affair in the full flood of the ROCOCO/BAROQUE, with a top

Late-17th-century gate-leg table

Hepplewhite hunting table

made of fossils. These are often semi-circular or some other shape on one side, flat on the other, and they were even made in JACOBEAN oak. Some of the ones you see with a marble top are probably VICTORIAN washhand-stands, but who on earth would realise that if you painted it?

Everyone always claims that a *Gate-leg* table saves space, but where do you put the chairs? However, they have been going a very long time now, from at least Stuart times, and have continued in manufacture by country craftsmen down to Victorian times. If you want an old one, you will have to pay for it, and

18th-century rent table

should buy it from a reputable dealer: for shoddy reproductions abound, as do fakes.

Something of an oddity is the *Hunting* table, sometimes called a *Wine* table, a long narrow semi-circle in shape, and sometimes with flaps at the ends to make it even longer. Some say they were intended for sitting around the fireside after dinner drinking port, others that they stood in the hall laden with what we would call snacks and drinks before the meet: I have seen them in auctioneers' rooms discreetly keeping you and me away from the rostrum. *Rent* tables are a special type, presumably used by stewards in estate offices, but with drawers all round: when rather deeper than this they become *Drum* or *Capstan* tables.

Our little three-legged affair is called a *Cricket* table, either because three legs equal three stumps, or because such a table was used on Hambledon Common – where the game started. But I have seen the name also applied to simple three-legged chairs without stretchers, so which is right? Anyway these are nice little tables. So, too, are the small round or octagonal *Tripod* tables, for tea: I got a late Victorian mahogany

Cricket table; 19th-century Manx table

one for only thirty shillings recently: it will be a pleasant substitute for the exquisite Hepplewhite and Sheraton affairs I can't afford now. The *Games* table is from REGENCY times, and I am afraid you will have to go to the expensive shops to buy any kind of them, except perhaps a chess table; don't be discouraged if the 'inlay' has gone – this can be put right.

Regency games table

What other tables are there? Small *Bedside* ones on a pedestal and with a drawer are comfortable things to have and can readily be found: *Worktables* with a pouch are getting harder to find, and so is anything *Kidney*-shaped. A *China* table with a fretted gallery round the top is a delightful thing to have, and there are lots of folding *Card* tables.

Anyone using the term *Refectory* table will, one hopes, realise that he either has a long oak farmhouse table of the last century, or a modern reproduction of something vaguely 'Elizabethan' or 'Cromwell' (see page 114). *Dressing* tables abound in the shops, for who doesn't want one? Useless here to look seriously at the creations of the eighteenth century, but not at all to turn over those of Victoria's reign, and even later. Especially, *Poudreuses*, or *Powder* tables, those delicious French affairs in rosewood and tulipwood with mirrors folding out of the drawers.

The bigger junk stores in the suburbs have some large, heavy but finely-made walnut and mahogany tables, with BOMBÉ fronts and lots of BAROQUE-ery, which are cheap, and *ought* to be convertible in some way. A type one often sees was popular about the turn of the century, in white-painted pine, often with cut-out shield-shaped or oval mirrors, and so many pleasant curlicues that one hesitates to associate it with the modern movement, although it is the anti-thesis of Victorianism. They were usually EN SUITE with tall wardrobes and wash-stands – when these latter have drawers and can be fitted with a mirror they can themselves make pleasant dressing tables.

Of course, *Dressing* tables can also be made up. The scarcity of *Sofa* tables already mentioned, suggests that they have been given a REGENCY mirror stand and turned to this use: much can also be done with a dwarf table and long mirrors. In fact the speculative eye can see many things of this kind – such as the long mahogany tables with stretcher and drawers: heavy perhaps, but sometimes there are light ones.

Victorian Loo table

Rather a drug on the market just now – and therefore game for the visionary – are all the round centre tables, once draped with their rich cloths of velvet and other materials. They were never meant to be seen, many of them, except with these drapings, which is why they look rather bleak: so perhaps we ought to put the drapings back. Alternatively we could go for one of the kind which has a decorative top: either covered with printed oil paper, or in slate painted with trompe l'oeil views (one went for ten pounds at a sale last year), inlaid with stones like marble, or green serpentine from the Lizard area; also 'Scrap' or *Scagliola* – i.e. irregularly shaped pieces of marble, granite, alabaster or porphyry in cement. Also circular in shape is the *Loo* table, the term then signifying one at which you played the game of Loo, a sort of three, four or five-handed whist with forfeits. Ours hails from Dublin about the middle of the century but is perhaps not unlike the one which Charity Pecksniff and Mr Moddle once wanted to buy, together with eight rosewood chairs.

Terra Cotta

I would give the finest Parian figure there is for one in terra cotta, especially if it has been left 'in the rough' to show the true nature of the clay. Called the 'sculptor's delight', it is said that Michelangelo used this material to work out ideas which he afterwards executed in marble.

The Victorians loved it, like everyone else, and have left us tobacco jars, vases, inkstands, mignonette boxes, ewers, garden pedestals, fountains, hanging baskets, and the rest. Sometimes they painted it in enamels, sometimes inlaid it with mosaics, sometimes part-covered it with 'majolica' glazes in rich colours.

Terra-cotta garden urn

Terra cotta simply means 'baked earth', and it is basic earthenware, varying in colour from ochre to pink or lobster red, but calling for a high degree of fineness; in ancient times it was used for plaques, tomb figures, urns, sometimes decorated with encaustic (baked on) colours.

Terra-cotta tiles still grace many public buildings, restaurants, pubs, municipal baths and old-fashioned dairies, and as these relics come under the house-

Terra-cotta wall tile by Blanchards

o

breaker's pick there will be many fine specimens offered to us in the junk shops. Our plaque is one of a set of twelve representing the months of the year, designed and modelled by W. J. Morris for M. H. Blanchard of Blackfriars, London.

If you want statuary in terra cotta the best, in my view, comes from France. A sculptor named Dalou has some touching maternal groups, some small, some almost life-size, in the Victoria and Albert Museum, and the handling shows a wonderful sense of the material. Small groups are to be found in the Marché aux Puces at no very great cost.

Tokens

There are coins, which are specialist collecting, and there are tokens, something quite different – and to my mind much more interesting. They are sometimes to be found in boxes mixed up with the more worthless sort of coin, buttons, and old bits of glass. If you have a taste for social history and bygone customs you will find them well worth looking for.

17th-century trader's and 18th-century
lover's token

First there are the traders' tokens. This was a sort of private currency created by local traders faced with a shortage of small change. This first occurred in the troubled days of the Commonwealth, when tradesmen issued their own pennies, ha'pennies and fardens, embellished with their names, or initials, often with their addresses, and in the case of a tavern, the sign. As well as circular ones, they could be square, octagonal, lozenge-shaped and even heart-shaped. About 20,000 were issued so it will take you a little time to collect a complete set.

This early crop was put an end to by the issue of the first regal copper coins by Charles II in 1672. But towards the end of the next century another shortage of copper coins led to a second outbreak of tokens, much more interesting and varied than the first. These reflected all kinds of local trades or activities: a Lowestoft token of 1795 shows bathing machines on the beach with the words 'Sea Bath': Buckingham tokens featured lace, and Leicester gloves; teazles used in the local trade appear in tokens from Ashburton. Sellers of books, boots, umbrellas, had their tokens, as well as owners of menageries, tea gardens, and other places of entertainment.

But apart from those intended as currency to be redeemed eventually at the place of origin however many hands they passed through (like the cheques which were said to circulate during the war to save income tax authorities the bother of too much accountancy), there were tokens apparently issued simply as advertisements, or for collectors to buy, as with special issues of postage stamps. They bear political slogans, commemorate current events, show local views and buildings, mythical and real persons of fame or notoriety, just like the pottery of the time.

There is also another, even more meaningful sort of token for the romantically inclined, and this is the lover's token. Some of them were specially struck for the occasion, evidently by admirers with means: but others are simply coins of the realm with one side rubbed away and bearing a very special message to a very special person, or simply with her initials and the quite sufficiently eloquent pierced heart or true lover's knot.

By the way, if you don't want your tokens to lose their value, don't polish them bright. PATINA counts here as well as anywhere else, so simply brush off the dirt and leave it at that.

'Tooth and Egg'

You will doubtless have come across whitish metal wares of obviously oriental origin, usually delicately chased, and mostly in the form of boxes, ewers, small coffee-pots, and above all, an odd-looking thing with a sort of periscope which is actually a Chinese tobacco water pipe. They can be bought for very little, as you can imagine, and yet a group of these pieces can look very attractive. I know a pub on the Bath Road where there is a shelf-ful of them, and the landlord will tell you that they need far less cleaning than silver.

Why 'tooth and egg'? Here we have one of those gorgeous confusions which are among the most exquisite joys of the collector. This time it is not the trade which has gone wrong – at least not much – but the scholars, for until quite recently – in fact until Mr Alfred Bonnin cleared the whole matter up in the 'twenties – this metal was known as *Tutenag*.

Obviously the trade *would* call it 'tooth and egg' – who could blame them? But *Tutenag*, as Mr Bonnin showed after sifting the records of it over several centuries, is merely zinc, a refined form of spelter used in Europe for cheap reproductions of sculptures. What everyone has called *Tutenag* is really *Paktong*, which is the Cantonese pronunciation of *pai t'ung*, or white copper – it has also been called that. It is an alloy of copper, nickel, zinc and iron, which rings like a bell.

Not only has it come here in the form of the articles already mentioned, but in the eighteenth century it was imported as a metal for the making here by persons as yet unknown of magnificent fire-grates, fenders, fire-irons, candlesticks and other items which often go quite unrecognised, and have even, it seems, sometimes been ELECTRO-PLATED in mistake for nickel-silver.

Toys

There is a certain sort of shop which is not exactly a junk shop in the sense that you look there for things which are, or might have once been, considered attractive to look at, but all the same has its customers. The stock includes boxing gloves, door handles, cricket bats, golf clubs, empty oil drums, field glasses, pram wheels (in great demand for go-carts), cameras, drain pipes, cigarette cards, bird cages, guns, and old electric light fittings. Women fly from these places in horror: but men love them, and spend hours considering how they might make striking use of something which can be acquired for a shilling. It is an excellent place, by the way, to replace those brand new tools left to rust in the garden – at a fraction of their original cost.

Boys and small children also like them, one of the reasons being that they often have a stock of old toys, battered, but often quite serviceable. I wonder that no Victorian genre painter has ever given us a picture of father and son in one of these shops speculatively turning over an old gipsy van or coal trolley and wondering if it could be knocked into shape again.

These old toys have a really surprising survival rate considering the rough handling they have had: one can only conclude that the best are still single-

Victorian toys

hand, and have been in a box in a cupboard ever since.

Anyway, there they are, if you look hard for them, the funny little 'penny tin toys' of all sorts. Those were the days of many sorts of children's 'cars', and these appeared in their miniature form, sometimes with horses galloping up and down on the wheel axles. Buses, hansom cabs, taxis, cars, even railway engines, look pleasantly out-of-date. Allied to these are figures on stands which you trail behind you on a bit of string; these Irish paddies and dancing girls jig about in an entrancing way.

Cardboard boxes sometimes contain the melancholy remains of a board game, but usually the board has been lost: jigsaws might tempt one but for the fear of missing pieces, and anyway the subjects are usually rather solemn and religious. Building blocks also tend to be rather holy.

If we are going mechanical there is sometimes one

of those tin Highlanders or guardsmen which on being
wound up move around sideways like Mr Jingle's
horse, frantically saluting everyone in sight. There are
mechanical barrel organs playing unrecognisable
tunes and Indian jugglers performing jerky tricks with
snakes. Some of these bear the letters DRGM. I
expect this means something about the Deutsches
Reich, but we always called it 'Dirty Rotten German
Make', though that didn't stop us buying them.

If instead of a hard-up-looking father and son, you
see a smartly-dressed business man hanging around
one of these shops, be sure he is looking for one of
those steam or petrol engines we had bought for us in
our early teens. I suppose these should be called models
rather than toys, but the business man wants to be
in the fashion and put one on his office windowsill, so
that he can remind himself that if his firm hasn't
made any other progress at least they're now using
electricity instead of steam.

Then there are the old magic lanterns, the kaleidoscopes, stereoscopes – how the present generation of
boys 'copped on' to these things when 'three-dimen-
sional' everything was the rage a few years ago!

Just occasionally you will see one of those marvellous butcher's shops with all those ribs of beef and
sides of mutton hanging outside, and the butcher in
his blue apron. (I never had one of these myself: is
it true for everyone that the toys one liked best were
those one was never bought?)

Lastly there are the soldiers, now no longer in those
fine big boxes with cavalry and infantry, tents and
stamped-out bushes and trees, but chucked in a box
and probably covered with chalk. I pick them up
sometimes and contrast them with the unbreakable
ones of today: no boy would ever want them, but

'Safety' rocking horse of 1900

for all I know I may be handling some great rarity of a hussar from Germany wanted by collectors all over the world. A good Noah's Ark I have not seen for a long time, but there are plenty of crude home-made ones.

As for the great rocking horses, with their studded saddles and flowing manes, these move quickly into the better-class shops for they make their money as decorations.

Trembleuse

Sometimes you may come across a cup and saucer of unusual design. The cup is two-handled and the saucer has in its centre a perforated gallery into which the cup fits snugly. This is a *trembleuse*, a word which will not make it very difficult for you to imagine the

18th-century Derby trembleuse cup and saucer

original user as being an old lady or gentleman with shaky fingers.

The earliest one I have seen came from Sèvres in about 1760; the most recent was a seaside souvenir made by, if I remember correctly, Goss.

Truncheons

Now and then you will see one of the old painted police truncheons. A collection of forty odd that came up for sale recently included about twenty painted ones, five showing the arms of George IV and one those of George III.

When people collect truncheons their earliest specimens are usually those of what you might call the opposition; being used by bad men, however, they were called cudgels or bludgeons. Some of these were pretty murderous things – there is one of twisted whalebone with a leaden head – so it is not surprising that the early watchman's staff was a very hefty affair, at least twice the size of a modern policeman's baton (the change in terminology is again instructing). The Bow Street Runner's weapon, the tipstaff, was a

Inn truncheon

badge of authority as well, and anyone who received it on the bonce got a right royal bruise the exact shape of the crown with which the staff was capped.

But people in those days had also to look after themselves, so you will come across truncheons which are nothing to do with the police. Private citizens carried them, inns kept them in case it became necessary to keep customers in order, many societies, like the Buffaloes, kept ceremonial ones: all of these would paint on their names and initials, sometimes very handsomely. Those which went in the above-mentioned sale averaged about a pound a piece, but, of course, those of historic interest would fetch much more than this.

Valentines

> *Tomorrow is St Valentine's Day*
> *All in the morning betime,*
> *And I a maid at your window*
> *To be your valentine.*

Valentines from York Castle Museum

Those romantic, playful, usually anonymous missives, got up in their pierced hearts, lacing and pink silk, which once appeared in their hundreds of thousands on St Valentine's Day, are having quite a revival at the moment. This makes one interested in all the old ones, which can sometimes be found in those inexhaustible boxes and albums in the back of junk shops.

Nobody seems to know which of the various St Valentines is the one celebrated on February 14, nor what connection he has with

> *Unnumbered lasses, young and fair,*
> *From Bethnal Green to Belgrave Square*
> *With cheeks high flushed and hearts loud beating*
> *Await the tender annual greeting.*

As will be seen by our quotations (from Shakespeare and Macaulay respectively) the tender traffic was a two-way one, this being the day when an approach was permissible not only from the man, but also from the maid – though Ophelia's lady perhaps went a little too far. It is probably no accident that the day coincides with the Roman Feast of the *Lupercalia*, in honour of Pan.

There always seems to have been some element of chance, or mystery, about the greetings, and when in the eighteenth century the first cards were sent, it was generally anonymously. The idea seems to have been that you were suddenly made aware of being adored by someone: who could it possibly be (as if you didn't know!).

From the first hand-written cards (words culled from textbooks) one moves to the first printed cards, appearing early in the nineteenth century, and decked out in embossed paper, velvet, lace, shells, leaves, even spun glass; and then to cards with scented sachets, edged with swansdown, cheques on the 'Bank of Love' (see CHRISTMAS CARDS). There is an excellent collection in the Castle Museum at York.

Two factors seem to have contributed to the downfall of the Valentine card until its recent revival; one, the emergence in the mid-nineteenth century of mocking ones, sent with deadly effect to those who had scorned you, or merely as crude jokes. The other was the fact that it paid manufacturers to concentrate on the CHRISTMAS CARD, which was used by everyone, not only lovers and haters.

Victorian Styles

By way of pulling together remarks offered here and there in this book it may help to mention a few of the astonishing terms used in talking of Victorian furni-

Victorian 'Etruscan' amphora by Battam & Sons

Victorian baroque sideboard

ture and other 'art manufactures'. It has already been noted how ADAM or NEO-CLASSICAL turned itself into REGENCY by grabbing, rather than deriving from, classical and exotic ideas like 'Grecian', 'Egyptian', 'Roman', 'Pompeiian', 'Etruscan' and so on. About the year 1830 there came the inevitable reaction, with an outbreak of what was called LOUIS XIV, but was actually a mix-up of BAROQUE and ROCOCO (*cf.* 'Revived Rococo' china as in Rockingham and Coalport). The furniture then made, in spite of its obvious difference from the real thing, is now avidly sought by the French. Following this, and under the influence of Scott's historical tales and the rest of the Romantic movement, we had 'Elizabethan', which, however, was much more like Restoration – note our 'Abbotsford' CHAIR. Not content with that the designers began ranging around among such styles as Byzantine, Lombard, Romanesque, Norman, Cinquecento and François Premier – to follow which would take us a long way outside the covers of this little book, more's the pity.

All these ideas chugged merrily along until about the time of the Great Exhibition in 1851, the manufacturers vieing with each other to fascinate the newly enriched but as yet untutored BIEDERMEIER classes. By then you find these themes embodied in almost everything, usually with a generous dash of what the

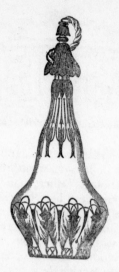

Enamelled glass decanter
with fuchsia motif

Mid-Victorian naturalism in gas bracket

Victorians, in their heart of hearts, really loved best of all: the faithful and painstaking reproduction of natural forms. Thus our decanter, with its fine 'Mahometan' (and typically Victorian) bulge below the waistline, but also a fuchsia motif in the stopper; and a brass gas bracket which doesn't stop at using the plant as a motif but disguises itself as a branch of it.

Similarly, our hall stand with good dog Tray offering harbour to umbrellas is 'a capital idea' and

Cast-iron umbrella stand

the ELECTRO-PLATEd teapot, considered a great technical advance upon Sheffield plate, neatly combines some naturalistic leaves with ROCOCO handle and spout and just a touch of GOTHIC about the trimmings. 'Its utility', we are told, 'suffers in no way from the quaint fancy of its form.'

Our ELECTRO-PLATEd inkstand, probably of BRITANNIA METAL, shows a good helping each of BAROQUE, ROCOCO and 'Renaissance'; also, in the Parian figure by Alderman Copeland, another pre-occupation of

Electro-plated teapot by Dixon & Son

the Mid-Victorians, the nude female form. This one, writes a contemporary commentator, 'nestling the dove, typical of Faith and protection, may haply tend to influence the feelings of those to whose use it may be devoted'. One hopes so, but with all those chained

Electro-plated inkstand
with Copeland Parian figure

Andromedas and Circassian slaves, sold in thousands
by the Alderman and Mr Minton and others, to say
nothing of our lady climbing up the umbrella handle
to reach her pumpkin and her bunch of grapes, one
wonders if this pious hope was realised. Still, there was
always a Victorian Elizabethan or LOUIS QUATORZE
piano to play on – this one was made by a Mr
Chickering of Boston, U.S.A. – a Victorian BAROQUE

Carved ivory umbrella handle

sideboard to carry that decanter of port wine or
Madeira, and a GOTHIC range downstairs for Cookie.

After all this mid-century fun and games with
styles there was a backward look at the straighter
lines of LOUIS XIV and ADAM, followed by glances at
Sheraton, Hepplewhite and Chippendale, all done
with the heaviest possible hand and straying far
away from the lithe grace of the originals, also lots

P

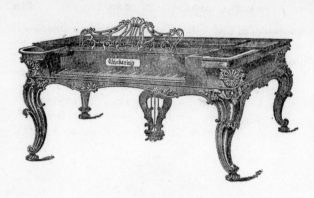

'Louis Quatorze' Victorian piano

of padding, needlework and leather. Towards the end of the century you had exotic imports like JAPANESQUE and the stock in the ORIENTAL DEPARTMENT, also the William Morris 'mediaeval' Arts and Crafts Movement, and, finally, ART NOUVEAU.

In all these things, however, there was an unmistakable Victorian handling and feeling; and much of this work, though greatly admired, found its way in a much watered-down fashion into the ordinary things of the time. These you will still see in the junk shops, solid, sometimes very comfortable, sometimes hideously not so, but always vital and always assured of itself and of the world it lived in. There *was* a Victorian Style, and you can have a lot of fun looking for it.

Electro-plated fish knife

Watch Keys

Those who like to collect in miniature might have a look at the watch key from before the days of the self-winding watch. Surprising though it may seem to those who have seen only one or two, these come in enormous variety, and many of them are quite beautifully designed.

Gold watch keys

In the early days of watches, the patterns of the watch keys followed those of clocks, but later they became very much more elaborate. Many reflect the beautiful work that went into the watches themselves, being engraved, enamelled, and often set with precious stones or Wedgwood cameos. Cut and polished steel, brass, pinchbeck, silver and gold were used, and some bear the emblems of different trades, or heraldic designs of one kind or another.

Watch Holders

Among the many small items which reflect in miniature the tastes of their time, and also the many sorts of material in which these were expressed, is the bedside watch holder.

Now that we wear wrist-watches one presumes that these things are no longer made: but once upon a time they were necessities. Upon retiring, you detached your gold hunter from its chain and hung it on

Victorian watch holders

one of these little holders, which stood upon the bed-side table; it could then serve as a clock.

Some of these holders in fact are so large and elaborate that one wonders if they did actually serve as clocks, perhaps housing a second watch, or one too large for the pocket, like a carriage watch. Most sought after perhaps are the elaborately carved ROCOCO ones in soft pearwood, many of them from France, which show workmanship equal to anything else in furniture at the time. These often have a figure of Father Time bearing the clock on his shoulders. Towards the end of the eighteenth century, as one might expect, they take on the more austere lines of ADAM, some in the form of grandfather or longcase clocks, or miniature swinging mirrors. These are attractive and so also are those in the forms of well-heads or garden temples, where the watch hangs from a hook in the centre. Sometimes you get a combined watch and trinket stand, or folding ones for travelling, or others carved in the form of houses or castles.

Apart from wood, polished or painted or perhaps with brass inlay, there are REGENCY examples in bronzed brass and other metals. In the same family, of course, are these watch pockets in BEADWORK, for hanging on the curtains or headboard, presumably for those who had no bedside table.

For those who hadn't a watch anyway there was always the Staffordshire chimney ornament in the form of a sham clock, with the painted hands perpetually at half-past one.

Wearmouth Bridge
The true name of a famous structure which, because it appears so often on Sunderland pottery, has become known to most people as SUNDERLAND BRIDGE; under which heading an account is given of the different versions of it.

Whatnot
What is a whatnot, and when is it not an ETAGÈRE? As I mentioned under that head there are some who claim that they are the same; and there are others who suggest that a whatnot stands on its own four legs, supporting two, three, four, or even more stages; whereas an ETAGÈRE stands on a sideboard of some kind. Those with a central pillar ought probably to be called dumb waiters (*v. Looking in Junk Shops*).

Whatnot

It is also for consideration that there is a difference of style. The word ETAGÈRE, it seems to me, has to connote something with a REGENCY or Empire flavour, or possibly something delicately Hepplewhite in acajou, its tiers soaring above a glass-fronted case at ground level: there may be handy little drawers below the shelves. Whereas a whatnot can be a matey affair in slender VICTORIAN mahogany, the tall ones for a bare corner, the short ones for your bedside. They are popular again, and so getting dearer all the time.

Whieldon

Occasionally you will see an octagonal plate with a tortoiseshell or mottled glaze which will be offered you as 'Whieldon'. Even a cracked one may command its thirty shillings.

This is a humble member of a very distinguished early Staffordshire class of pottery which is identified with the name of Thomas Whieldon, perhaps the most famous of those potters, like John Astbury, who made the entrancing figures in dripping coloured glazes – musicians, bandsmen, horsemen – which make enormous prices in the salerooms today. But although Whieldon developed these glazed earthenwares in association with his apprentice and partner Wedgwood, he also had a hand in most of the other Staffordshire wares of the middle and late eighteenth century, especially saltglaze, creamware and Jackfield ware (red pottery covered with a black glaze and gilded). Josiah Spode was another of his apprentices.

Wicker Ware

Everyone surely remembers the comfortable creak with which one sank into a wicker chair or settee:

Wicker chair and settee 1900

and how cool they could be in summer, and cushiony comforting in winter. Here they are, both of them *aetat* 1900.

When was basketwork first used for these comfortable fat affairs? Some say about 1880 or 1890, but the experts help us little with such humble things. Perhaps their history goes back a very long way indeed, like that of the wicker or basketwork cradle which one can see in prints of the seventeenth century.

Today one sees the plain ones lingering in junk shops; but those gaily painted ones, or those with different coloured osiers interwoven to make patterns, have they all gone to the bonfire on Guy Fawkes' night?

William and Mary

This is one of the most interesting of our periods, for it marks, not only what is called the Age of Walnut, but also a pretty complete break with JACOBEAN. Dutch William brought Dutch influence, notably BAROQUE splendour, but also prepared the way for the elegant simplicities of QUEEN ANNE.

The Cabriole leg appears, an inverted cup (see LEGS AND FEET), also the Tallboy, together with seaweed marquetry and tall book-cases on the top of the

William and Mary table

various kinds of writing desks. Note the serpentine legs and stretchers on this burr walnut side table, made about 1690. Dressing tables, lots of cabinets with lots of drawers, much lacquer, walnut veneer – and the China cupboard. This was not yet for Chelsea and Bow, but for Chinese blue and white or FAMILLE VERTE (a little early for FAMILLE ROSE) porcelain. The delftware would have been in the dining-room.

Wine Coasters and Wagons

If you get worried about your wine bottles making a mark on the table, you can of course buy one of those handled basket things in which the bottle reclines. But I have always felt that these are clumsy things which can make the wine slop up and down in the bottle, and even all over the tablecloth.

I much prefer the coaster or stand, an item of table ware with a long and respectable history. Bottles in the eighteenth and nineteenth centuries, especially the heavy 'sealed' ones mentioned in *Looking in Junk Shops*, had rough bottoms, and if anyone asked you to slide it along the table the chances were that you would score the wood. Hence the round or octagonal stand of silver mounted on wood, perhaps entirely of silver,

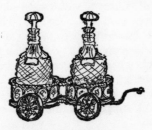

Double decanter carriage

or Sheffield Plate, some of them very handsome with their pierced galleries. Decanter stands are wider and shallower than those for the bottles, at any rate in the nineteenth century.

After the stands, the wagons or carriages. It evidently occurred to somebody that a more elegant way of sending round the wine than shoving it along would be to put it on wheels: so you had that pleasant thing, the pair of double wine wagons with shafts. Those who still prefer shoving can buy a coaster in the shape of a boat.

18th-century silver wine coaster

Wine Coolers

This can still be a useful article about the house, and so many people have discovered this that they are no longer very cheap to buy.

This is a pity, for I personally detest what happens to a bottle of Pilsner or white wine when it is kept in a refrigerator as though it were milk. These drinks need to be cold, but not frozen, and our Georgian and Victorian ancestors knew better than to invent something which made it necessary for them to wait for their drinks to become drinkable. There are even *publicans* who keep their lager in refrigerators: garrotting, I suppose, is the only really adequate punishment.

But these wine coolers, with their iced water, are

Late-18th-century wine cooler

just the job: what is more, they look well in any company of furniture. I like the brassbound ones, used in taverns, with their capacious depth in which you can submerge the bottle completely: the early-eighteenth-century ones were rather shallower, being designed for the 'dumpies' of the time.

Those who like to do their drinking in an outhouse, away from all the female clatter, might like to know that William Kent, the great architect of the English BAROQUE, provided his houses with stone ones: it used much less ice. Which brings up a point that people are sometimes curious about: how did they produce ice in the eighteenth century? The answer is that they collected ice in the winter months and stored it in ice-houses underground.

APPENDIXES

Museums

Some Specimen Foreign
Pottery and Porcelain Marks

Reading List

Museums

All haunters of junk shops can cultivate their taste and inform their eye by using the museums. Years ago, when these places were dark stuffy holes where stuffed bears jostled fossil cases with illegible labels, 'museum' was almost a dirty word – you went there to meet a girl, or if it was raining. Today, a new race of curators has taken the land. They understand that the purpose of a museum or an art gallery is to be interesting and instructive and above all pleasurable; and so they have learnt to display things, to organise special shows, to entice collectors to let their pieces out for a public airing. Many of them have had the enterprise, too, to concentrate on their own local industries and crafts, so making detailed studies of them generally available.

Here, then, are a few suggestions about collections which might interest you. I have listed them according to place rather than subject, because although you know where you are, you may not know what interests you until you see it. It is an entirely arbitrary choice; for a complete list with times of opening, etc., see the annual publication *Museums and Galleries in Great Britain and Northern Ireland* (Index Publishers, London), a most helpful guide. For that other kind of museum, which some prefer, the home made available to the public, see *Historic Houses and Castles in Great Britain and Northern Ireland*, from the same publishers.

BEDFORD   Cecil Higgins Museum. Admirable collection of eighteenth-century porcelain and glass.

BIRMINGHAM   City Museum and Art Gallery. Almost everything, but particularly, for us, porcelain, silver, and local nineteenth-century glass; also (at Newhall St) local manufactures, e.g., small arms and steam-rollers.

BRIERLEY HILL, Staffs.   Museum and Art Gallery. Fine collection of Stourbridge and Continental glass, excellent reference library, and most enthusiastic and helpful staff. See also STOURBRIDGE while in this area.

BRIGHTON   Art Gallery and Museum. Fine and practically unique 'Willett' collection of Staffordshire pottery figures, etc. Also Sussex ware. Thomas Standford Museum at Preston Manor has interesting Edwardian/Victorian interiors.

BRISTOL   City Museum and Art Gallery, Queen's Road. Fine local (and Nailsea) glass, delftware, Chinese and English porcelain. Also Blaise Castle Folk Museum, Henbury.

BURY ST EDMUNDS   Remarkable Gershom-Parkington Memorial Collection of Clocks and Watches, 8 Angel Hill. Informative and chatty curator.

CAMBRIDGE   Fitzwilliam Museum, Trumpington St. Collection of national status, especially porcelain, slipware, delftware, glass, sculpture, pictures. A delightful museum, most helpful about photographs. See also Folk Museum, Castle Street.

CARDIFF   National Museum of Wales, Cathay Park. Another national collection, especially interesting for Welsh porcelain, pottery, Pontypool ware. Vast hidden reserves of Morton Nance Collection of Welsh ceramics available for serious students. Staff most helpful in every way. Old mining machinery outside. Go also to Welsh Folk Museum at St Fagans.

DERBY   Museum and Art Gallery, Wardwick. Fine Derby porcelain and Chesterfield brownware.

EDENBRIDGE, Kent. Chiddingstone Castle. Japanese lacquer, swords, other oriental and Egyptian items, in 'Gothick' castle.

EDINBURGH   Museum of Childhood, 34 High St; Lauriston Castle, Cramond Road South (Blue John, Wool Mosaics, etc.); Lady Stair's House (Scottish pottery). Several other fine museums and galleries.

GAINSBOROUGH   Gainsborough Old Hall, Parnell St Folk Museum, especially needlework.

GLASGOW   Several fine museums, especially Kelvingrove Art Gallery and Museum (arms and armour, ship models); also Tollcross Museum *for* Children, and Old Glasgow Museum, People's Palace (period domestic life).

HARROGATE   Royal Pump Room Museum. Fine collection of Leeds pottery.

HASTINGS   Public Museum and Art Gallery, Cambridge Road. Sussex and Kent pottery and ironwork.

HIGH WYCOMBE   Art Gallery and Museum. Chairs, especially the Windsor, Buckingham lace.

HONITON   Honiton and Allhallows Museum, High
St.   Honiton lace, etc.

HOVE   Museum of Art, New Church Road. Fine
period rooms, glass, china, embroidery, etc.

LEEDS   City Art Gallery. Fine Leeds and Staffordshire pottery. Abbey House Museum, Kirkstall.
Admirable   folk   museum,   reconstructing
streets of houses, shops, workrooms, viz: pottery
(with the old Leeds moulds), tobacconist, tin-
tack maker, Italian warehouseman, ironmonger, claypipe maker, wheelwright, saddler,
blacksmith, weaver, tanner, toy seller, haber-
dasher, apothecary, watchmaker, musical
instrument maker, pub with landlord's private
parlour upstairs. In galleries, Anglo-Saxon to
Edwardian costumes, children's toys, games
and books, doll's-house furniture, glass, china;
4,000 books on chimney sweeping; musical
instruments;   lighting   appliances;   walking
sticks; treen; Britannia metal, etc.; pottery.
A wonderful threepenn'orth.

LONDON   There are over one hundred museums
in London and suburbs, among which may be
mentioned:
Bethnal Green Museum – especially costumes
and dolls' houses.
British Museum – everything.
Geffrye Museum, Shoreditch – period rooms.
Ham House, Richmond – Stuart furniture.
Horniman Museum, Forest Hill, S.E. – musical
instruments and absorbing ethnographical
collections.
London Museum, Kensington Palace – social life,
cradles, costume.

National Maritime Museum, Greenwich – ship models, instruments, medals.

Percival David Foundation of Chinese Art, Gordon Square – magnificent Chinese porcelain.

Pinto Collections of Wooden Bygones, Oxhey Drive, near Northwood – 5,000 specimens of treen.

Tower of London – armour, uniforms.

Victoria and Albert Museum, South Kensington – probably finest collection anywhere of porcelain, glass, pottery, metal, applied art of all kinds, especially jewellery, swords, silver, sculpture, Chinese, Islam, and European art. Fine photographic and slide library, lectures; also you can take your things there for identification (though not valuation).

Wallace Collection, Manchester Square – fine art generally, especially Sèvres porcelain, miniatures.

MANCHESTER Many fine museums, including Gallery of English Costume, Platt Fields, Rusholme – over 1,000 complete dresses, and 2,000 accessories.

Whitworth Art Gallery, Oxford Road – prints, drawings.

NEWCASTLE-UPON-TYNE Laing Art Gallery for local eighteenth-century glass (especially Beilby) and Slagware, also other local industries.

Museum of Science and Engineering, Great North Road – engine and machinery models.

NORTHAMPTON Central Museum and Art Gallery, Guildhall Road. Footwear through the ages.

OXFORD Ashmolean Museum of Art and Arch-
aeology. Fine Worcester porcelain, glass,
Roman and medieval pottery and glass,
coins, prints.

Museum of Eastern Art.

Museum of the History of Science – instruments
and apparatus.

Pitt Rivers Museum – handcrafts, ethnological
items – you can spend hours here looking at
bygones from all over the world.

PETERBOROUGH Museum and Maxwell Art Gallery.
Local things, including French prisoners'
straw marquetry work.

PLYMOUTH City Museum and Art Gallery. Especially Plymouth and Bristol porcelain.

PORTSMOUTH Victory Museum, H.M. Dockyard.
Ship models, figureheads, Nelson relics,
etc.

PRESTON Harris Museum and Art Gallery. Interesting and well-cared-for collection of
Victoriana. Enthusiastic curating.

READING Museum of English Rural Life, 7 Shinfield
Road. Agricultural and rural bygones.

SHEFFIELD City Museum. Cutlery, Sheffield plate,
Britannia ware.

STOKE-ON-TRENT City Museum and Art Gallery,
Hanley. Unique collection of Staffordshire
pottery and china.

Wedgwood Museum, Barlaston. Factory's collection of early wares: you can see it still being
made.

STOURBRIDGE Fine collection of Stourbridge glass in the Hall of the Council Offices. Nice to see these unique pieces, but at risk of exacerbating local rivalries one wishes they were in the public collection at BRIERLEY HILL.

SUNDERLAND Museum and Art Gallery. Sunderland lustre and ship models.

TUNBRIDGE WELLS Museum and Art Gallery. Tunbridge ware and bygones.

WOLVERHAMPTON Municipal Art Gallery and Museum. Bilston enamels, pottery, japanned tinware.

WORCESTER Perrins Museum. Worcester porcelain and china. Enthusiastic and expert curator. The whole story of Worcester potting and a walk round the factory afterwards.

YORK Castle Museum. Folk museum with cobbled street, shops, etc., as at Kirkstall. Magnificent collection of bygones, also crafts, costumes, toys, in nearby Debtors' Prison.
Railway Museum, Queen St. Locomotive and railwayana.

SOME SPECIMEN FOREIGN POTTERY
AND PORCELAIN MARKS
(For British Marks, see *Looking in Junk Shops*)

AUSTRIA
Vienna

BELGIUM
Tournay

DENMARK
Copenhagen

FRANCE
Chantilly

Clignancourt

Limoges

Marseilles (Faience)
Veuve Perrin

Paris (Potter)

Paris (Samson imitating
Meissen)

Quimper

Sèvres

GERMANY
Berlin

Dresden (*Royal Factory, Meissen*)

Dresden, Helene Wolfsohn, from 1860's imitating early Royal Mark

Dresden, Helene Wolfsohn, from 1880's ('Crown Dresden')

ITALY
Capo di Monte

Le Nove

Nove

Reading List

This brief list adds a few specialist titles to the much longer and more basic one given in *Looking in Junk Shops*. Some titles will still be in print but older ones must be sought in the second-hand bookshops or the libraries.

The Story of Picture Printing in England during the 19th Century, C. T. Courtney Lewis.

History of Christmas Cards, George Buday (1954).

Maps and Map Makers, R. V. Tooley (1949).

British Fire Marks, B. Williams (1934).

History of Old Sheffield Plate, Fred. J. Bradbury (1912).

The Miniature Collector, G. C. Williamson (1921).

Rings, G. F. Kunz (1917).

Potteries of Sunderland and District, James Crawley (Sunderland Museum, 1960).

Sussex Pottery, J. M. Baines (Hastings Museum, 1948).

Royal Lancastrian Pottery, 1900–1938, A. Lomax (1957).

19th Century Cameo Glass, Geoffrey W. Beard (1956).

Victorian Porcelain, Geoffrey A. Godden (1961).

The Medal Collector, Stanley G. Johnson (1921).

Seals, W. de G. Birch (1907).

Children's Toys Throughout the Ages, L. H. Daiken (1953).

Trade Tokens, W. Boyne (ed. G. C. Williamson).

Book of Chessmen, Alex Hammond (1950).

Truncheons, E. R. H. Dickens (1952).

Handicrafts and Industrial Arts of India, Rustum J. Mehta (1960).

Japanese Handicrafts, Yuzuru Okada (1956).

The English Home, Doreen Yarwood (1956).

Old Furniture for Modern Rooms, Edward Wenham (1951).

Encyclopaedia of Furniture, Joseph Aronson (1938).

Decorative Art of Queen Victoria's Era, Frances Lichten.

Victorian Comfort, John Gloag (1961).

ABC of Japanese Art, J. F. Blacker (1908).

ABC of Indian Art, J. F. Blacker (1911).

Chinese Art, Judith and A. H. Burling (1953).

Piqué: a Beautiful Minor Art, Herbert C. Dent (1923).

English Victorian Jewellery, Ernle Bradford (1959).

Handbook of Antique Chairs, Carl W. Drepperd (1908).

English Cream-coloured Earthenware, Donald C. Towner (1957).